apartment buildings, classrooms), creating, in juxtaposition with the book's earlier poems, a striking montage of real and imagined events.

More overt growth in Brodsky's style is apparent in the third book in the volume, *The Foul Rag-and-Bone Shop*, originally compiled in the spring of 1967 but expanded in late 1969. Its highly symbolic, imagistic pieces range from diffuse, surreal depictions of events in the socially and politically turbulent 1960s to focused reflections on universal themes like faith, love, and justice. Heightened by provocative accounts from the author's own life, this diverse book ultimately shows not only his willingness to experiment with forms and topics but also his work's increasing maturity.

Together, these three books chronicle the personal and professional growth of one man, but more importantly, their poems provide insight into the human experience and evoke a timelessness making them as relevant today as they were decades ago.

A must for Brodsky enthusiasts and collectors!

THREE EARLY BOOKS OF POEMS BY
LOUIS DANIEL BRODSKY
1967–1969

**Missouri Center
for the Book**

Missouri Authors
Collection

Books by LOUIS DANIEL BRODSKY

Poetry

Five Facets of Myself   (1967)* (1995)

The Easy Philosopher   (1967)* (1995)

"A Hard Coming of It" and Other Poems   (1967)* (1995)

The Foul Rag-and-Bone Shop   (1967)* (1969)* (1995)

Points in Time   (1971)* (1995) (1996)

Taking the Back Road Home   (1972)* (1997)

Trip to Tipton and Other Compulsions   (1973)* (1997)

"The Talking Machine" and Other Poems   (1974)*

Tiffany Shade   (1974)*

Trilogy: A Birth Cycle   (1974)

Cold, Companionable Streams   (1975)*

Monday's Child   (1975)

Preparing for Incarnations   (1975)* (1976)

The Kingdom of Gewgaw   (1976)

Point of Americas II   (1976)

La Preciosa   (1977)

Stranded in the Land of Transients   (1978)

The Uncelebrated Ceremony of Pants Factory Fatso   (1978)

Birds in Passage   (1980)

Résumé of a Scrapegoat   (1980)

Mississippi Vistas: Volume One of *A Mississippi Trilogy*   (1983) (1990)

You Can't Go Back, Exactly   (1988)

The Thorough Earth   (1989)

Four and Twenty Blackbirds Soaring   (1989)

Falling from Heaven: Holocaust Poems of a Jew and a Gentile
   (with William Heyen)   (1991)

Forever, for Now: Poems for a Later Love   (1991)

Mistress Mississippi: Volume Three of *A Mississippi Trilogy*   (1992)

A Gleam in the Eye: Poems for a First Baby   (1992)

Gestapo Crows: Holocaust Poems   (1992)

The Capital Café: Poems of Redneck, U.S.A.   (1993)

Disappearing in Mississippi Latitudes: Volume Two of *A Mississippi
   Trilogy*   (1994)

A Mississippi Trilogy: A Poetic Saga of the South   (1995)*

Paper-Whites for Lady Jane: Poems of a Midlife Love Affair   (1995)

The Complete Poems of Louis Daniel Brodsky: Volume One, 1963–1967
   (edited by Sheri L. Vandermolen)   (1996)

Three Early Books of Poems by Louis Daniel Brodsky, 1967–1969: *The Easy
   Philosopher, "A Hard Coming of It" and Other Poems,* and *The Foul Rag-and-
   Bone Shop (edited by Sheri L. Vandermolen)*   (1997)

Bibliography (Coedited with Robert Hamblin)

Selections from the William Faulkner Collection of Louis Daniel Brodsky:
A Descriptive Catalogue   (1979)

Faulkner: A Comprehensive Guide to the Brodsky Collection
    Volume I: The Bibliography   (1982)
    Volume II: The Letters   (1984)
    Volume III: *The De Gaulle Story*   (1984)
    Volume IV: *Battle Cry*   (1985)
    Volume V: Manuscripts and Documents   (1989)

Country Lawyer and Other Stories for the Screen by William Faulkner   (1987)

Stallion Road: A Screenplay by William Faulkner   (1989)

Biography

William Faulkner, Life Glimpses   (1990)

Novels

The Adventures of the Night Riders, Better Known as the Terrible Trio
(with Richard Milsten)   (1961)*

Between Grief and Nothing   (1964)*

Between the Heron and the Wren   (1965)*

Dink Phlager's Alligator   *(novella)*   (1966)*

The Drift of Things   (1966)*

Vineyard's Toys   (1967)*

The Bindlestiffs   (1968)*

* *Unpublished*

Louis Daniel Brodsky
(ca. 1967)

THREE EARLY BOOKS OF POEMS BY
LOUIS DANIEL BRODSKY
1967–1969

THE EASY PHILOSOPHER
"A HARD COMING OF IT" AND OTHER POEMS
AND THE FOUL RAG-AND-BONE SHOP

Louis Daniel Brodsky

12/30/07

St. Louis, M

EDITED BY
SHERI L. VANDERMOLEN

TIME BEING BOOKS
POETRY IN SIGHT AND SOUND
St. Louis, Missouri

Time Being Books®
10411 Clayton Road
St. Louis, Missouri 63131

Time Being Books® is an imprint of Time Being Press®
St. Louis, Missouri

Time Being Press® is a 501(c)(3) not-for-profit corporation.

Time Being Books® volumes are printed on acid-free paper, and binding materials are chosen for strength and durability.

ISBN 1-56809-030-7 (Hardcover)
ISBN 1-56809-031-5 (Paperback)

Library of Congress Cataloging-in-Publication Data:

Brodsky, Louis Daniel.
    Three early books of poems, 1967–1969 / edited by Sheri L. Vandermolen.
        p.   cm.
    Contents: The easy philosopher — "A hard coming of it," and other poems — The foul rag-and-bone shop.
    ISBN 1-56809-030-7 (cloth). — ISBN 1-56809-031-5 (pbk.)
    I. Brodsky, Louis Daniel. Easy philosopher. II. Brodsky, Louis Daniel. "A hard coming of it," and other poems. III. Brodsky, Louis Daniel. Foul rag-and-bone shop. IV. Title.
    PS3552.R623A6   1997
    811'.54—DC20   96-17150
                                                                  CIP

Cover photo courtesy of the author
Book design and typesetting by Sheri L. Vandermolen
Manufactured in the United States of America

First Edition, first printing (July 1997)

ACKNOWLEDGMENTS

Sheri L. Vandermolen, Managing Editor of Time Being Books, is credited with presenting each poem in this volume in its most definitive and polished form. Her editorial skill and her passion for exacting perfection from the English language have given these poems a clarity I could only have dreamed they might achieve when I composed them three decades ago. Listening to their rejuvenated voices will always remind me how deep are the measures of my awe and appreciation of her.

My thanks also go to Jerry Call, Editor in Chief of Time Being Books, who has read this manuscript and improved it with his insightful suggestions.

I also wish to make grateful acknowledgment to these publications, in which the following poems, in different versions, have appeared: *Free Lance* ("Confinement," "Designs in Storm Time," "Land of the Setting Sun," "Mass Hysteria," "Mulatto," "Selma, Alabama, 3/6/65," "Tenement Eyes," "Unmatched Ecstasy," "Winter Seminar," and "Zoo"); *Reflections* ("Awakening," "The Burning Off," "Do Not Disturb," "Dr. Johnson's Rain," "Jan's Song," and "The Seer"); *Elephant & Castle* ("Land of the Setting Sun" and "Mulatto"); Ball State University *Forum* ("Morning's Companion"); *Byline Magazine* ("Season's End"); *The Literary Review* ("Visitation"); *The Web* ("Winter Seminar").

Three poems, "Jan's Song," "Election," and "Zoo," were originally published in 1968 by the University of Tennessee as part of a musical score composed by Gary Nelson entitled *Three Motets on Poems by Louis Daniel Brodsky*.

These books have also been published individually by Time Being Books, and the poems (with the exception of "This Pendent World," "Indian Summer," "Morning's Companion," "Song," "Cycles," "Phantasms of Sleep," "The Nuptial Bower," "The Turning In," "Introit," "FDR Drive and 78th Street," "The Devil's Circus," and "Visitation") are included, chronologically, in the Time Being Books publication *The Complete Poems of Louis Daniel Brodsky: Volume One, 1963–1967.*

CONTENTS

FOREWORD *by Sheri L. Vandermolen* *xv*

THE EASY PHILOSOPHER
1967

ONE

The Questions *27*
Sortie *28*
The Uprooting *29*
Mother Earth *30*
The Vanity of Human Beauty *31*

TWO

Zoo *35*
Night Watchman *36*
The Sport of Winds *37*
Mass Hysteria *39*
Memphis: The Conflagration *40*
Mulatto *41*
Squall *42*
Tenement Eyes *43*
Summer Idyll *44*
The Prodigal Children *45*
Season's End *48*
Temporary Stay *49*
Grandfather to Himself *51*

THREE

Winter Seminar *55*
The Trial of a Retiring University Professor *56*
A Tended Vastation *58*
Seminar in Symbolism *59*
April Seminar *62*

FOUR

Epitaph   *65*
Valediction Forbidding Despair   *66*
Do Not Disturb   *67*
Five Facets of Myself   *69*
Boy of Fits   *70*
Confinement   *71*
Election   *72*
Storm: A Dialogue   *73*
Up from Exile   *75*
Dr. Johnson's Rain   *76*
Caddy's Sin   *78*
The Seer   *79*
Jan's Song   *81*

FIVE

Epiphany   *85*
Curse   *87*
Repulsion   *89*
Expulsion   *90*
The Quick   *92*

"A HARD COMING OF IT" AND OTHER POEMS 1967

A Hard Coming of It   *95*
Essie   *100*
Heading North from Friday   *101*
Unmatched Ecstasy   *103*
Student Prince   *104*
Boats Against the Current   *108*
Loomings   *110*

Inquiring Adam   *111*
The Withheld Sensibility   *112*
Ritual   *113*
The Hunters and the Hunted   *114*
Suggestions of Demise in an Occasional Professor
    of Modern Poetry   *116*
Keep the Fires Burning   *117*
Cottage by the Gulf   *119*
Selma, Alabama, 3/6/65   *120*
Exigencies   *122*
Hobo   *124*
Designs in Storm Time   *125*
The Gathering In: March Ides   *126*
A Wintering Mimosa   *127*
The Abiding   *129*
The Strangler   *131*
Shall Rise Again   *134*
Another Mother   *135*
Reductio ad absurdum   *136*
Prince of Cigarettes   *137*
Legacy   *138*
Exalted Thought   *139*
Narcissus   *140*
Clyde Griffiths' Chrysalis   *147*
[Morality gapes through the bars,]   *148*
Beginnings   *149*

THE FOUL RAG-AND-BONE SHOP
1969

This Pendent World   *155*
The Foul Rag-and-Bone Shop   *156*
Indian Summer   *157*

An Anatomy of the Believer: The Twenty-Sixth
  Anniversary   *158*
Morning's Companion   *160*
A Newer Consummation   *161*
Song   *163*
Zealous Voices   *164*
The Achieve Of   *165*
Cycles   *167*
Phantasms of Sleep   *168*
Ishmael   *169*
The Nuptial Bower   *171*
The Turning In   *172*
Taps   *173*
The Burning Off   *179*
Introit   *181*
FDR Drive and 78th Street   *182*
The Well   *183*
The Personal Creation   *184*
Land of the Setting Sun   *187*
47th Street West   *189*
Awakening   *191*
The Devil's Circus, Chicago, '68   *193*
Good Friday, 1965. Riding Westward   *194*
Visitation   *199*
Rejection: The Legacy   *200*
Morning Rush Hour   *202*
The Accomplishing   *203*

FOREWORD

Louis Daniel Brodsky composed his first poem in 1963, as an undergraduate at Yale, and went on, during his early years as a writer, to author hundreds of pieces of both poetry and prose. By the summer of 1967, when he launched his professional writing career, he had gathered his best poems into four books, three of which are presented in this volume (the poems from 1965 to June of 1967 are also comprised in *The Complete Poems of Louis Daniel Brodsky: Volume One 1963–1967*).

He completed his inaugural book of poetry, *Five Facets of Myself*, in January of 1967, while pursuing his Master of Arts in English at Washington University, in St. Louis. Although he had assembled two booklets of his poems in years prior (*Ever-Becoming Dreams*, a set of eight poems compiled and mimeographed in 1964, at a boys' camp in Lake Nebagamon, Wisconsin, and an untitled group of seven poems, referred to as *"Zoo" and Other Poems*, created one year later at Lake Nebagamon), *Five Facets* represented his first book-length manuscript. Having included some of his favorite, most revised poems in the *"Zoo"* booklet, he borrowed its full contents and selected forty-three additional poems he had written between 1965 and 1967 to form the text of *Five Facets*, which he divided into five thematically arranged chapters.

The first sections of the book, which draw heavily from Brodsky's trips to Illinois, Wisconsin, and Florida, depict various segments of society, sometimes through characters' perspectives but more often through the author's autobiographical voice, which resonates throughout the work. His encounters with the culture and values of rural Midwestern towns, described in the poems "The Prodigal Children" and "Designs in Storm Time," among others, foreshadow themes of the heartland and small-town life he would develop years later, as a resident of Farmington, Missouri, and turn into two full-length books, including *The Capital Café: Poems of Redneck, U.S.A.* Brodsky's experiences in his native St. Louis are recorded here also, in poems like "Mass Hysteria" and "Tenement Eyes," as are his travels through racially conflicted cities further south, represented in both "Memphis: The Conflagration," and "Selma, Alabama, 3/6/65." In addition, the latter poems indicate the beginnings of the love-hate relationship he would develop with the South in years ahead, which would eventually precipitate an entire series of Mississippi poems and culminate in his creation of *A Mississippi Trilogy: A Poetic Saga of the South*. His fascination with Florida and the symbolic cycle of death and rebirth he found there took root at this time as well, starting with *Five Facets* pieces like "Student Prince," "Confinement," and "Vision" (later called "Election") and ultimately resulting in dozens of Florida poems and the in-progress manuscript *Floridian Idylls: Poems of Fort Lauderdale*.

The early chapters of *Five Facets* also present Brodsky's contemplation of his personal life, delving into his roles as a student, a writer, and a camp counselor. Juxtaposing the responsibilities of adulthood, exemplified in poems like "Season's End" and "Keep the Fires Burning," and the pressures and expectations of youth, expressed in "April Seminar" and "Winter Seminar," these first sections contrast Brodsky's awareness of the practical knowledge awaiting him in the world at large with the sense of subjugation he felt in the classroom setting. And by blending actual events from the camp and university with fictive ones, chapter by chapter, the book constructs a hybrid world of real and imagined experience unique to Brodsky. He would revisit this realm of his youth decades later, recalling his summers at Lake Nebagamon with nostalgic hindsight and reliving them with the mature insight of a middle-aged adult through his son's own adventures, when forming the book *You Can't Go Back, Exactly*, containing fifteen of his poems written about the camp during the 1960s and early 1970s as well as fifteen later ones, nine of which he wrote as a parent of a Nebagamon camper.

The final chapters of *Five Facets* return to Brodsky's role as a student but more abstractly so, relying on his knowledge of literary references and his application of various authorial voices. He was influenced by a wide range of writers, including Dante Alighieri, John Milton, Samuel Johnson, and William Faulkner, as evident in poems like "Up from Exile," "Inquiring Adam," "Dr. Johnson's Rain, 1750" (later titled "Dr. Johnson's Rain"), and "Caddy's Sin." But although he emulated several styles, the poems in this portion of the book reveal that he was continually searching for his own voice and pondering the writer's function in society, as in "Five Facets of Myself" and "Do Not Disturb."

Determined to better his work, Brodsky continued revising the poems in this book for months but also began compiling a new manuscript, *The Foul Rag-and-Bone Shop*, which originally contained seventeen poems written between 1965 and 1967. These pieces, although not divided into chapters, present several of his recurring subjects, with surreal descriptions of trips to Florida ("The Foul Rag-and-Bone Shop" and "The Burning Off"), glimpses of city life ("Morning Rush Hour" and "47th Street West"), and reflections on concepts like faith and justice ("Rejection: The Legacy" and "Zealous Voices"). But they also show an expansion in the author's style: he was reaching further into the world and deeper into the mind of the writer than ever before, as seen in poems like "Taps," "The Personal Creation," and "Good Friday, 1965, Riding Westward," which evoke socially and politically biting tones still prominent in his poetry today.

Brodsky finished the initial version of *The Foul Rag-and-Bone Shop* in the spring of 1967 but subsequently set it aside, not creating its expanded edition until the fall of 1969. Instead, still not fully satisfied with *Five Facets*, he returned to its text and chose to reconstitute it into a new book of poetry, *The Easy Philosopher*, to which he apportioned the final typescripts for thirty-three of the *Five Facets* poems. He completed *The Easy Philosopher*, the first book in this volume, in June of 1967, following his graduation from Washington University.

Although he added only eight other poems to the body of *The Easy Philosopher*, he rearranged all five sections from *Five Facets*, reordered the poems, removed the part titles, and revised nearly every piece, giving the manuscript a wholly different structure than its precursor. Using this reorganization to emphasize the advancement of his style, he left only one *Five Facets* poem ("The Questions") in the first chapter of the book, moving the others and replacing them with four of the eight new poems, all of which were composed in May and June of 1967. He inserted another new poem ("Squall") in part three, and to highlight the texture these later pieces provided, he placed two others ("Epitaph" and "Valediction Forbidding Despair") at the beginning of the fourth chapter and one ("The Quick") at the end of the book. He made the addition of this final poem more significant by changing the short, Miltonic section four of *Five Facets* to section five of *The Easy Philosopher*, giving the book a powerful closure, with a more abstract, reflective tone, focusing on man as the human animal who questions his existence, a theme still prevalent in his work. Another of his current subjects, the Holocaust, originated at this time as well, in "Valediction Forbidding Despair," laying groundwork for poems that would surface twenty years later and eventually burgeon into five books dedicated to the topic, including *Gestapo Crows: Holocaust Poems*, in which the revised form of "Valediction" appears.

Having earned his degree in St. Louis in May and preparing to move to San Francisco by September to participate in a creative-writing program at San Francisco State University, Brodsky sensed an urgent need to collect into book form the rest of what he considered his most advanced work. Since he had already assigned two thirds of the *Five Facets* poems to *The Easy Philosopher*, he allocated the remaining third to a new manuscript, supplementing them with fifteen additional poems composed from 1965 to 1967, to yield *"A Hard Coming of It" and Other Poems*, the second book in this volume.

Unable to devote much time to the full development of *"A Hard Coming of It" and Other Poems*, Brodsky created only one bound copy of the book, with no contents page, dedication, or chapter designations. And although the poems from *Five Facets* had undergone much revision, most of the other poems had only limited drafts, especially those from 1967, which were written and revised in short spans of time, such as during his trip to Redington Beach, Florida, in January and during breaks in his school schedule in the spring.

While the six poems from 1965 and 1966 that were augmented to the text echo Brodsky's previous themes and subjects, including events at camp ("Exalted Thought") and at school ("Reductio ad absurdum"), the nine poems from 1967 reveal how his poetry had evolved by that time, with his embrace of a broader purpose: to record everything, minutiae included, in the world around him. These pieces reach into daily existence to register the poet's natural environment (trees, rivers, storms, seasons), as seen in "The Gathering In: March Ides," "A Wintering Mimosa," and "The Abiding," as well as his immediate surroundings (parks, stores, streets, apartment buildings), such as in "Narcissus," "The Strangler," and "Clyde Griffiths' Chrysalis."

Brodsky finished revising these poems and the others in *"A Hard Coming of It" and Other Poems* by the end of June of 1967, approximately one week after completing *The Easy Philosopher*, and began to concentrate his efforts on his prose writing, intending to become a professional fictionist once in San Francisco. He generated few poems in the months to follow, and from the summer of 1967 to the summer of 1971, he produced only one complete volume of poetry, the second edition of *The Foul Rag-and-Bone Shop* (leaving a separate manuscript, *Points in Time*, which he started piecing together in 1968 and 1969, incomplete for decades).

Thus, his poetic growth slowed dramatically in 1968, a year he spent romantically, emotionally, and professionally unsettled. After receiving his

Master of Arts in Creative Writing in the spring, he headed to Lake Nebagamon for the summer, where he composed a handful of camp poems, and then traveled to Coconut Grove, Florida, in late August, where he went to embark on a teaching career at Miami Dade South Junior College and to be with his college sweetheart, Jan Hofmann. However, disturbed by the turmoil within himself, by the political climate of the country, and by the misgivings he felt during the first days of his teacher orientation, he began to reconsider his decision to dedicate himself to the pedantic, "political" world of academe. Within weeks, he resigned from his position and returned to Missouri to pursue a career anchored in practical experience.

Back in St. Louis, in an attempt to bring stability to his personal and professional life, Brodsky started working at a men's-clothing factory, owned by his family, in Farmington, Missouri, which had a population then of approximately ten thousand. Living in a motel during the week and commuting to St. Louis most weekends, he was not able to keep a regular writing routine, and although he purchased a home in Farmington in the spring of 1969, he still traveled to St. Louis frequently to diminish the sense of isolation he felt.

By the fall of 1969, having established himself in his job and heightened his romance with his future wife upon her return to St. Louis, Brodsky renewed his poetic efforts and generated the expanded edition of *The Foul Rag-and-Bone Shop*, the third book in this volume, adding to the text twelve poems composed between the summer of 1967 and the summer of 1969. These later poems, written while he was traveling and developing his first serious relationship, reflect his increasing maturity and the emotional growth inherent in his experiences with love, portrayed in "Song" and "Morning's Companion." A few pieces from that period also reveal his need to explore his pensive, skeptical side, as in "This Pendent World" and "The Devil's Circus, Chicago, '68," which he wrote in August of 1968 in response to the social and political unrest he had witnessed in San Francisco and Miami.

Although this expanded version of *The Foul Rag-and-Bone Shop* ventures beyond Brodsky's first years as a poet and into his time of personal and professional transition, it is included in this volume of "early" books of poems because it represents the author's final vision for a manuscript he originally shaped during his apprentice years, within the same period as *The Easy Philosopher* and *"A Hard Coming of It" and Other Poems*.

The poems of all three books, as they are presented here, have been corrected to meet Time Being Books' current guidelines for language usage and mechanics, with spelling changes, alterations of punctuation and capitalization, and all other grammatical corrections added silently. However, in order to preserve Brodsky's early writing style, his use of idiosyncratic British spellings and archaic spelling variations has been preserved as has his intentional use of neologized words and compounds. The editorial changes are meant to standardize the work and enhance its readability, without any relineation or substantive revision, and they have been made only under the direct supervision of the author.

Sheri L. Vandermolen
10/11/95
Morton, Illinois

THREE EARLY BOOKS OF POEMS BY
LOUIS DANIEL BRODSKY
1967–1969

THE EASY PHILOSOPHER
1967

To Jan,
I dedicate these two quiet years of my life.

ONE

* This symbol is used to indicate that a stanza has been divided because of pagination.

‡ This symbol is used to indicate that a piece is incomplete.

The Questions

Where is the secondhand,
Duco-blue Buick
That cluttered the oak-strewn street
In front of my youth?
Where is the half-timbered,
Brown brick, two-family flat
And the fort made of twigs,
Maple sticks, and a pinespear floor,
The Kenilworth of our backyard?
Where are the vacant spots:
The makeshift ball lot,
The basement haunts
Where the six of us
Plotted heroics of a hearsay Bluebeard
Or angry Genghis Khan?
Where is the church I feared,
The priest, who preached hell, I hated,
And the rebellious Dedalus I became?

And where is my mother,

Her blue felt beret,
The long gingham print,
And funny little leather shoes
With buckles that blinked like doubloons?
My memory has misplaced them
Among the clutter of mounting years.
It only remembers the questions now,
And the hum behind the eyes grows louder;
The awful buzz in the ears
Is persistent.
Yet the tongue no longer resists
The Eucharistic wine;
The stomach accepts the softest bread,
Craves the palpable feast.
Perhaps I am going dead,
A loose bulb
In a dim, immolated cellar,
Licking fine, forgotten preserves.

Sortie

Bristles of a searchlight's broom
Scratch the night with nervous strokes.
Though clouds attract its sweeping beam,
The sky stays whole, annealed, and clean,
For the pendulum's consistent twitch.

The pilot flies a piece of flak,
Tracking doubts that besiege his mind.
Fear attacks him through her sights.
The man explodes in a moment's flame.
Night remains broken, bloody, unclean.

The Uprooting

He is both sexes, self-perpetuating,
A limp erection injecting itself.
He has thrived in the womb he cocooned
After thorough investigation. Parasitic,
He chose this room for himself.
He was this room; his inaudible voice
The choice that moved no other earth
Than that which threatened to doom him
Where he lay in terrigenous cloisters.

Now floods rage above his civilization.
Sounds that compound his heartbeat
Grow dim inside him. Walls give way.
All fortifications are inconsequential.
As he climbs out, his lungs pump air
Too pure to sustain his squatty body.
The end rushes up to defeat him.

The precipice toward which he gestures
Refuses his suicidal ascent.
As he concludes an inward journey
From the scruffy pit of his guts
Through symmetry where neck joins head,
A man within the animal stands up,
Surveys his passage out of the bowels.
He squirms, curls, sinks to surface mud,
A sluggish creature in an alien terrain.

Mother Earth

The Earth Goose,
Most obtuse mother of all,
Shows wrinkled features,
Tobacco nose,
No shoes on her feet.
She has so very many children
No one knows what to do
But retreat
        In need of new soles.

The Vanity of Human Beauty

The mirror through which she peers
Undresses her. A dying reminder
Of nosegays pressed between pages
Rivets her flesh to the glass.
Outside, naked silhouettes pass.
Ghosts who have never known retreat
Reach up to touch her fleeting glance,
Kneel down in gutters to weep.
The secret she keeps discovers her.

Two

Zoo

A peal of recorded trumpets
Introduced King Arthur,
The trained chimpanzee,
While the California sea elephant
Vied for top honors
Before my avid eyes.
He was slick sensuality,
Glued to the pool's green lip
Before slipping away into coolness.
Behind me,
The sloth bears
Ogled at paid customers
For signs of recognition.

Everything was talking
In singular ascendancy.
Visitors sneaked up on cougars
In cages, their own naiveté
Obvious as steaming manure.
Cowards fingered venomous triangles
Poised behind glass,
And lovers held hands,
Shying from Freudian implications
In the reptile station.

I could see the whole zoo
Looming before my lurid eyes
Like the grand spectacle
In the Caracalla *Aida*.
But the zoo was friendly,
I thought,
In its own private way
On that May afternoon,
When solitude stalked me,
Uncaged.

Night Watchman

I let down the guard;
Cigarette smoke
Bombards my lungs.
I can do nothing to avert
The inevitable dispelling of dreams
They leave me to sweep away.

I am a speck of nighttime,
Carrying an everlasting sconce
Like some maddened Macbeth.
I travel feckless and bored
Down tenement corridors
Where no pilgrims stir.

I am no gallant chevalier
But Arthur,
The night watchman,
Dangling a ring of keys
That hold no secrets
Along their nubby spines.

I protect all but myself
From this screaming silence.

The Sport of Winds

People that march with slogans and things tend to take themselves
a little too holy . . . it's pointless to dedicate yourself to the cause;
that's really pointless. That's very unknowing. . . . People who can't
conceive of how others hurt, they're trying to change the world.
They're all afraid to admit that they don't really know each other.
— Bob Dylan, interviewed in *Playboy*

A cold gust of wind
Rushes across my neck.
The hair on my naked skull
Flutters recklessly
As Illinois wheat,
While I shy
From the group that gathers
Before my suspecting eyes.

Indiscreet slogans
In praise of freedom and right
Pass regimentally.
Vulgar soles,
Rebels of some darker cause,
Scatter the pebbles
Demosthenes spat.

Cardboard posters,
Erect,
Church steeples
Of some newer religion,
Ride the backs
Of identical Christophers;
They bob in impious genuflection,
Reflecting the same reflections,
Projecting a simple, subtle safety in numbers.

There are people there,
Somewhere
Beneath those cardboard scepters.
They wear their consciences
Nakedly as lesbian witches
Gyved to broomsticks, riding westward
Into night's dry vagina.

And I sit here freezing,
Braced against this greystone bench,
Reasoning
How people huddled in human clusters,
So tight-lipped,
So heavy-lidded (their eyes sewn shut),
So sculpted and alone,
Can believe in darker causes
That, like wasted semen,
Grow rancid in pools of misconception.

Mass Hysteria

Pondering the Percy slaying,
9/18/66

It's that damn black cat again,
Spanning neighborhood window ledges
When all but few have settled in bed.
Who belongs to that fictive miniature,
That little leopard licking night's foggy paws,
Watching drunks slobber home alone?
There ought to be a law! Superstition
Shouldn't be allowed out on all fours.
"Someone forgot the door latch, that's all.
He'll come home. You just watch and see.
No need worry yourself sick," she'd say.
"People know a cat . . . wouldn't you agree?"

Prowlers go on the loose,
Combing unlikely districts for girls
In nightcoats and innocent breasts.
There's unrest in this place,
Where disgrace prates like eunuch satyrs.
There's no room in here
For queers disguised as messiahs.
Be gentle, baby! That's all I say.
If you're going to club skulls
And stab eyes, like gigging frogs,
Pick on deep-sea fish and dinosaurs,
Things that don't exist anymore.

It's that damn black cat again,
Posing coquettishly as a German whore
Behind the window where I lie in bed.
I wonder is anything abreast out there,
Where footsteps breed maggots
On the floor of my restive ears?
I hear car squeals
And the roar of diesels far away
In cellars where dreams of myself
Huddle like children in air-raid shelters,
And I wonder does this gangrene darkness
Really divide day from night?

Memphis: The Conflagration

For Gene Redmond

Memphis by night.
That's how I remember it,
Driving north to south:
One gaping mouth of neon
Fillings and wisdom cavities
That needed extraction.
I reacted to the salivating night
Like an Italian beggar
Distracting passersby
With operatic gestures of penury.

Memphis by rainy night.
That's how I remember it.
My windshield wipers smoothed away
Soft revisions of the city,
Metronomically.
Swirling car smoke
Soothed my impatience, my comic hatred.

Memphis by Negro night.
I remember it that way, too,
Scuttling along my sightless eyes
Like a naked, soft-thighed chimera.
I stopped my frightened car
Long enough to watch
Lightning spray the town
With revenge. I was Nero.
I started my silent engine
And drove into the flamerainy night.

Mulatto

Hair the color of applesauce,
Mottled with cider streaks;
Hazel eyes that blinked like freckles
Under the sun's spectacle.
The grass she lay facedown in
Licked her stomach
With feline tongues.
She watched her twenty-one years
Pass overhead
Like migratory ducks in flight,
Remembering the cold kisses
That chased her tragic escapes
And hot rumors
That greeted her arrival
In each new place.
Her fingers were stained
Green and wet
Where she tore clots of grass
Aimlessly
From the ground's wrinkled face.
Tomorrow looked at her
With albino eyes
And a disconcerted brow.
Now she was sobbing,
Resisting her separateness,
Her inconsequential disgrace.
Somewhere, a thrush throated
Three quick notes,
Then dissolved in the underbrush.
She stood up naked,
Alert to night's sneer,
Ready to flee again
Into a thousand hungry mouths
Of the populace.
As she neared,
Her footfalls echoed
Like pulsebeats
In the city's groin.
She was up for sale
To anyone who could match the price
Of her ambivalent nudity.

Squall

For Jan,
in June

Wind beats the winter wheat.
Cornstalks not two feet old
Inflate rippled fields,
Flap in the stippled breeze
Like people clapping hands
In a crowded coliseum.
Cows turn their backs to the world.
Sows leave off feed troughs
To huddle against weathers
That twist the swifts' course,
Knot a freight train's whistle,
And buckle the very air
That bridges spoke-taut cities
And these flat-out plains.
Now rain paints war designs
On the face of this plow-traced land.
Furrows retreat like sandcastles
Washed by a truculent sea.
Autos creep wheel-deep in water.
Traffic lights blink into sleep.
Against one window of the restaurant
Where we, just passing through,
Have been forced to serve the storm,
Debris etches a dance of death.

Tenement Eyes

Raped noise,
And boys return home from growing up.
An alley cloyed with tilted music,
And naked shouts
Shatter the lids of night.
I can see her privacy
Through venetian slats,
Grown riotous there,
Where her pink, silky skin
Swallows his lust
Hastily.
Now I shrink away from the sill,
Unrelaxed,
Into rude hexagonal breathing.
The eyes go limp,
Dreaming of past retreats,
Drowning in lewd chastity.

Somewhere, a black saxophone
Scratches lazy elegies
Over taut frets of the skyline.
A cat brushes up against space,
Arches, barely mewing.
Prurient dawn licks red the horizon,
And I awaken, seeing it all.
She sleeps, a selfish, simple face,
Subtle reduction to the commonplace.
Now they are one again,
Lying there defenselessly,
Free in stupid harmony.
My eyes creep along the alley's backbone,
Searching in vain,
Craving their myriad, stray, unsown seeds,
Still seeking (the eyes),
Sneaking back now, returning,
Fatigued and alone.

Summer Idyll

For Jan,
in Jacksonville

Outside her den window,
Autos moved slowly uptown
Through heat-filled streets.
Elm, sweet gum, and maple
Swayed with Illinois breezes.

Within, a Victrola's silhouettes,
Like acrobats walking wires
Stretched from New Haven
To the taut Old World,
Barely touched our ears.

We were a staid couple
Lifted from some family album,
Winslow Homer's society people,
Fragile Japanese figurines,
Deftly playing croquet,
Flitting across boardwalk lawns.

Then something changed the symmetry.
Rural masques grew dim
Beyond the window's perimeter,
And bustlebusy Piccadilly
Sifted dateless grains
Through our hourglass eyes.
We saw the Mississippi River
Pause, then dissolve
Into Thames' quivering lips.

The Prodigal Children

For Jan,
in May

The headless horseman,
A yellow sports convertible,
Flees dawn's gaunt apparition,
Whines down country strips,
Ripping May's fifty degrees
Like hands a plastic bag.
The car, a goblin,
Slides stroboscopically
Past wallowing sows' eyes,
Beneath laundered skies
That withhold impatient heat.

We race away,
Distancing the city's silvery ghost,
Pacing ourselves against no-clocks,
Erasing imaginary blocks of time
That contain people
In White Cross.

We flee that city
Retrogressively,
Not just beyond clipped lawns
And planned littlehouses
But by immediacy
Itself,
Into a past that thrives
Like ancient taboos.

And at once,
A blink discloses
One,
Then manifold billboards
Fading under a feverish sun
That never knows defeat.
But the eyes know
What the mind has yet to see:
An ancient civilization just ahead,
Growing, still, in its tired soil.

Penshurst, if you please,
Up 67
As the buzzard flees:
Statuary lying colossal
As cast-iron lattice work;
A town gone stale as pastry
Left overnight behind glass;
A lukewarm remnant
In time's subsiding womb,
Locked in custom
And dislocated
Like toys children leave
In backyard lots
When they slouch into manhood.

Am I the kind old florist's son
Or one of the local druggist's boys?
Is she
Who rides with me
Some slatternly, late-night
Blanche DuBois
Or careless Caddy Compson
Come home
Embracing pointed calumnies
To see a nameless child?

Now, day's blue noon
Sprays pavements that glister
With silverquartz.
The Square stares at us
From four angles
Like carneyqueer mirrors,
Distorting self-conscious perspectives,
Filling narrow-slender minds
And plump-squat bodies
With unknowing glimpses of themselves.
We see them seeing us,
Striding easy,
Eyeing windows lined with vapid dreams
That come from newer worlds.
We are the freaks here,
Children who wear their namesakes.

It's the children. They escape
The gartered constriction
Parents wear about their brains;
They flee inculcated complaints
To seek out richer societies
Beyond the furrowed fringes
Their own fathers sow with soy
And barley seeds.
Cultivation bears no relation,
In their impatient minds,
To wheat thrashers
And co-op combines.
Perhaps this accounts
For the lapse in sensibilities.

But we've returned, now,
To confront the source,
To abide with invisible remorse
That breeds in bib overalls and boots,
That goes helling Saturday nights
And bends the spirit of Sunday
Like strongmen lifting rubber weights.

We have come home with ourselves
Intact,
Practical pilgrims
Who know the virtues of slow change,
No change.
We'll crusade against elm disease
And things like that.

Season's End

For "Muggs"

Trunks piled high as shipping crates
Await stevedores.
Dust-swirling cabins are vacant
As discarded pepper tins;
Their screen doors
Creak in the rain's imperious face.

The boarded-up rec hall
No longer reeks of hot meals
Or feels the dizzy weight
Of children milling, spilling drink
Over hardwood floors
That wear scars of two-score years.

The boys are going slowly
Down brown-rusty tracks,
Cracking barriers
Where birch ends
And the easier scent of poplar and ash
Is lost in diesel exhaust.

We who waved at the station
Take up the highway home,
Seeing in each fleeting town
The same boys running down hills
Where we don't stand, anymore,
Waiting to check their graceless descents.

Temporary Stay

We approach the slow city,
Cloaked like a sleeping princess
On the lip of a hill;
Neither of us cares what witch
Fixed that throat-clogged apple.
Imagination's constancy,
The mind's timeless antic,
Subdues the necromantic spell.

Twinkle-fuzzy lights
Blink far out,
Tiptoe over the lake's wizened face.
Beacons go red, then null,
Their voices noiseless as dog calls.
Here in the harbour,
Hulls that know no stopping
Resist the channel's chop till dawn.
But we'll be gone
Before those high-shouldered tankers,
Wands that Moses never knew,
Crank Cyclopean props
And veer obliquely from the shore,
Parting waters of a thousand ports.

Now we drive home,
Alone as unknown pioneers
Leaving disappearing traces
Behind twin-braced Conestogas.
The smoothbellied bridge
Climbs higher than ever before,
And grain elevators, oar docks
Float in tilting retrograde.

We are those lights
On the hilled horizon
And the ships moored tightly
With perishable lines.
We are that raucous cascade of sound
That came bounding, tripping, winding wild
Across the ears' invisible spines.

As we head home, our eyes,
Clocks that forget to remember,
Filter out uneven shades,
Tear with incommunicable surprise.
Ragged grass and roadside eyes
(Coon, deer, and peregrine cats)
Scatter before us
Like illusive thoughts that poets have.

We've entered the city and returned
With another of those treasures
That lie just ahead
Each somehow-, somewhere-tomorrow,
Awaiting only our discovery.

We will never forget
Duluth,
When strangled some other where,
Under copper-colored fahrenheits
Of sulphur-covered air
Or in the ruthless mangle
Of pitiless cities,
Locked in some other when.

Grandfather to Himself

That's a strange place to keep perfume
And a vanity mirror . . .
In the kitchen window, I mean,
Where you can't see me seeing you
Fastidiously estimate your features
While I eat across the way each evening.

I don't mind your radio screaming
Or the slow odors of meat
And bread that settle like phoenixes
In this yardstick corridor separating us.
Who would notice the noises, perfumes
Any other season than this hot summer?

Drawers slam; plasticware shares space
Where the breeze should be,
And I just sit here, staring nowhere
Particularly.
Yet I bet if Alice were here,
She'd say something. I just bet she would.

That highway out there . . .
It can really scare a person
With so much insomnia.
Doesn't it ever just want to quit?
That jet overhead on the roof . . .
I wonder where it's going.
If Alice were here, I bet she'd know.

This heat . . . so sticky. If I could drink,
I'd take a single shot of whiskey,
Iced.
She always liked it that way. . . . Say,
Where is she? Alice? Want a whiskey, dear?

I can hear them across the way,
Playing tag, kick-the-can.
Wonder who'll lick her perfume,
Whose room she'll lie naked in tonight.
Those kids . . . they'll be frightened. What about . . . ?
Who'll tuck them into bed, douse the lights?

Alice would say, "Who cares anyway?
When will you learn to concern yourself
With me? You be the homebody I married,
Not a monkey that gapes and stares at others."
Where are you, Alice, my sweet?

Maybe those kids'll ring my bell.
I'll tell them lore, mystery stories.
I have a brand-new carton of bubblegum.
They never come anymore. Not since Alice . . .
Who'll rinse their dishes, put them to sleep?
There I go again. I should think about myself,
Keep my mind off things that don't concern . . .

God, but it's hot! If tomorrow's like this,
I'll . . . Alice? Is that you crying inside me?
In whose room tonight? . . . A brand-new carton . . .
God! Let me sleep tonight and dream of children
And Alice and ice-cream cones, or I'll . . . I'll . . .
Anything to forget how little is little, being alone!

THREE

Winter Seminar

One tries to decipher
Three-day-old symbols
On the greenwhite blackboard.
Another, with nimble, yellowstained fingers,
Contemplates filtered disease,
Reads Donne's "Obsequies."
A third, more prudish yet,
Peers through the fearful symmetry
Of octagonal pince-nez.
She,
A brilliant vixen at twenty-three,
Could just as easily be
Winslow Homer's schoolmarm
In some one-room conception of the universe.

How intellectual and subtle we are,
"Doing" John Donne or scanning
The bricklayer's sonne
In our seminar class,
While I just sit here,
Mind too bleary to concentrate,
Imagining distractions that fit my temper
(Trying to spell Yoknapatawpha)
Beyond the window's grating.

Outside, it's begun to snow,
And I feel an urge to bolt,
Fleeing without my coat,
Arms and ears bare,
To touch one slow-exploding flake
And hear it sear the palm
As it disappears
Incarnate.

The Trial of a Retiring University Professor

His hollow-echoing feet
Follow treads of stoic tribunes
Who paced forums of oldest Rome.
The feet retreat repetitively
Through April's grey rain,
Down daylong corridors
From outside into the cave.

I, an intellectual heretic,
Stare at the taffy-pulled face
Of this academic mastodon
From the age of Eakins and Twain,
Waiting for his tired words
To stir two hours of dust.

His gullcolored hair
Refuses the room's heat,
Stays matted as morning grass;
The sodden mustache withers
Like drooping dog tails.
A scent of nicotine trails hands
That grasp at stray passages,
Friends without faces, sepulchered
Among disarrayed stacks of books.

His eyes, opaque fishbowls,
Grope for marginal notes,
Ghosts slinking in dark closets,
He made ten years ago.
Fraught with serious doubts,
He thumbs through yellowed pages
That crumble to his touch.
He fumbles, stumbling over words
That decimate his upstaged thoughts.
Wondering whether rescue will come
To his distressed memory, he asks,
"Are there any questions before I begin?"
A mutual pause embarrasses silence,
And he feints, boxing imaginary shades
That stand between him and his class.

Now the voice that knew Thoreau,
Emerson, and Edgar Poe
When he was still young enough
To be their grandsons' age
Breaks from his sacred notes,
And nine heads turn deferentially
Into his lips to listen.

"Why crave immortality
Just to outlive longevity?
Don't you know the Struldbruggs,
Lotus-eaters suffered their whims?
Why avoid those who sneeze
Or squeeze the grapefruit dry
Each morning before driving to work
Downtown? Why read hidebound books,
Whose authors read Juvenal, Democritus
Vicariously? Pleasure denies the intention.

"It's the pure intent, the furious pulse,
That makes death worth living for.
Eat the leopard's liver if you must.
Superstition is the best there is
For those who lack courage,
And religion without tradition
The best for those with convictions
Of their own temporality.
Morality, like the Holy Word,
Must be reinterpreted each tomorrow
According to the transfigured sorrows
And myths we create ourselves.
Crave the mortal in living!
Its grave lies out in the open,
Waits on nobody's dying humilities."

A Tended Vastation

Two pigeons
And a pearl-whorled squirrel
Scampered for acorns
And spiny blades of grass
On a shaded campus lawn.

These public fowl,
The cache-collecting scavenger
Went unseen by students
Crossing the green
On their way to share
Higher, well-deep secrets,
Hour after fetid hour.

Earlier,
I'd heard the black mechanic
Crack a rotor's motor,
Break the bracken air
Beneath a passive classroom.

Some studied agreement
Must have been made
By men for man
Himself
To rend seeds, emulsify leaves,
Unsightly things that breeze
And dog-eared days
Refuse to do away with
Gratuitously.

Yet
Who could ever guess
What intimacies
These ignorant creatures
Wrested from the ground,
Where the black hands,
Guiding the thrasher's scythes
From his parch-patterned paths,
Left a quay of Octobering grass?

Seminar in Symbolism

Monistic fusions of word and world
Swirl through my tired brain,
And I start to fade from the instructor's voice.
The eyes droop as in a child's blush;
The green floor rushes into my head.
"SPIRIT FLOWS THROUGH THIS MORAL EARTH."
Four cigarette butts define divinity
Beneath my feet, and I feel the linoleum's
Green-streaked whitecaps
Seeping comfortably into my skin.
Waves, light as webs, weave and roll,
Shrouding a school of white leviathans,
Four of them, swimming, killing real men.
(Hostile signs of divinity. The fusions:
Contradictions in terms. Symbols of sperm
And darker than jet.)
"SYMBOLS ARE OBJECTS
THAT STAND FOR SOMETHING ELSE,"
He reads from cryptic notes
Jotted ten years ago last Tuesday.
The ears hear pens running obliquely,
Squeaking over nine lined notepads,
Leaking under burdens of profundity.
The one who speaks behind my ears
Pauses, shuffling his tarot pack,
Listening to Ishmael tell Melville
About the moment of perception.
(Ah, difficult recognition . . .
Significance in all things . . .
Knowing and doing: the links of meaning.)
"MAN IS A SYMBOL-MAKING ANIMAL,"
He intones, insisting on heuristic fictions.
My eyes are spectators at the race,
Whose goal is a verbatim tape.
(The truth captured: an animal caged
For Sunday displays in an April park.
It's all the same cliché, though darker
In some climes than in others.)

"THE WHALE IS SYMBOLIC OF EVIL AND HATRED."
Chairs with eyes and ears sit straight
Before the T-shaped table in this booth,
Straining to hear each intonation:
Attentive arbiters of thought and truth,
Whose duty is to reconcile evil
In the human heart, mete out justice
To the whole or any of its literary parts.
"AHAB SOUGHT THE WHALE. THE WHALE IS EVIL.
ERGO, AHAB WAS AN EVIL BASTARD."
But the fusions deny syllogistic intrusion,
And I see the self and its universe
In endless search. Now Melville and Poe
Run below me, atop the sea's rutty crests,
Spanning interstices of history. The seas
Run more mysteriously. Bells ring through mist,
And I watch the mizzen listing
To lee shores alive with Elmo's fires.
(There's no safety there, where destruction
Bewilders lemmings and slow black cobras.)
Dark waves fragment darker horizontals,
Pitching the slipshod *Pequod*,
Like God the fallen angels,
Out of sheltered vaults of darkest night.
"SYMBOL IS AN OUTWARD SIGN
OF SOME INWARD STATE OF THE MIND."
I sit balking, I an animal stalked,
Not stalking, whimpering into his busy ears,
"But was the evil not there before?
And think if Ahab had brought safely into port
That blubberbooty boat? Yes, I can see them,
That crew, dicing for pieces of eight,
Gold doubloons, clothing, rusty harpoons —
Temples filled with blubber changers."
(Evil lurks in the heart of the process,
And the reverse hides ambiguities.)
Through the flaxen web, I see spiders;
One among them, the one-legged arachnid,
Drags the body's bilious personality
Along wharfs of Bedford and Nantucket,
In search, still seeking the universe
Behind the web's masked patina.

"SYMBOLS RARELY CARRY A ONE-TO-ONE . . ."
A cough. Now the prolonged five o'clock bell,
And I awaken, filled with imagination's depressant,
Rationality.
The bloodless foot shuffles cigarette butts
(Mere dirty dross of human nervousness),
And slat-back chairs cease creaking,
Go dumb as museum pieces,
Objectified.
And I am I,
Shaking out the eyes' dusty blankets
Past nine other sets of numb spectacles,
And each is of a similar species:
Students whose pens have dashed out marathons,
Dragging lagging sensibilities behind their scribble.
The voice erupts: "I SEE OUR TIME IS UP TODAY.
NEXT WEEK, BE PREPARED TO DO *WALDEN*."
The room darkens, the species lumbers out,
And the door goes closed against slow vacuum,
While heavy sighs stay locked in stale demise.
Outside, the city sun sinks through roofs
Of tight-eyed office buildings
As I walk to the car,
Dreaming of dinner and an evening cigar.

April Seminar

The legs pain;
The brain lags like cold butter
On steaming toast
In this once-a-week room.
Here, one discusses "myth";
Another,
Who knows the Fool,
Fusses over Cuchulainn
And the moon's silver fruit,
While I sit mute,
Cringing intellectually,
The hand hiding suspect yawns.

Oh, that I were Oisin,
Driving some fast machine
Past country lawns
Where poetry flows
Harsh as a muffler's vibrato,
Soft as gears slipping smooth
Through tamed mathematics.

Then alone,
Released by ungoverned speeds,
Would the heart tremble,
The eyes grow wild,
Flinging tears that smear
A million ragged sunsets.

FOUR

Epitaph

Life at stalemate:
An end anticipated
So long ago
That now
Even memories are in white.

Valediction Forbidding Despair

This summer is Treblinka;
Its regimental months
Are maws that caress us
In bloodless custody.
Victims, like crickets
Scratching dryness from limbs,
Chant hymns from lips
Which shape the air
With unfinished kisses.
Musicians and carpenters
Guard darker silences
Of those who crowd naked
In boxcars and chambers
Where perfumed night descends.
Memories race down chutes
To steaming graves
Obsequious few ply with balm.

Yet
Minds are excused from spirit.
The end obliterates nothing
But flesh
And the temporary wish
To rest.

Do Not Disturb

He twitches a muscle,
Switches positions in his chair,
Secretly winks an eye
Now and again
To itinerant gods passing by.

He spends hours on fetid end
Scouring compendiums,
Writing letters he never seals,
Sealing thoughts and hard-fought insights
Onto a typewriter's roller
He never threads with paper.

When the air goes stale
In his shelf-lined museum
Of signed limited editions,
He draws open the curtains,
Pulls the scroll-rolled shade,
And lifts a winter-long window
To sniff the uncertain air.

The days stay fixed for him out there,
Where the screen locks limbs
Like tape stuck loosely to its mesh.
But those trees seem dimmer than usual today,
The sky shimmers myopically in his eyes,
And he thinks how things resist change.

He sees past the crippled mimosa,
Through plastic-coated magnolia fronds,
Toward a duck-filled pond nearby.
But these are decoys left intact
After ten tedious winters he's seen;
They still bob aimlessly
When wind ruffles their balsa backs.
And there, a red-painted, plaster-casted,
Lackluster pickaninny
Fishes the neighbour's arithmetical lake.

He sees this same scene changed slightly
Every day, each season, by the moods
He brings to his study from sleep.
*

It's here, in steeled states of calm,
He finds relief from all that was
And might just be were he to leave
For half an hour's emergency.

But he finds life most interesting
In desk drawers only he can unlock
With keys he hides discriminately
Or when thumbing through dog-eared copies
Of Lockean philosophy
While relighting cigarettes
Abandoned in moments of creativity.

But just now, he seems at loose ends.
Something has stopped him dead to rights.
It's the quiverless trees, the unshrill air,
And the silence filing through the screen
Like legions of insane driver ants.
He sees the silence coming in funnels
Toward the desk at which he sits,
And he listens, as a dog might
From conditioned fright,
To hear these insistent echoings.

The ringing behind the ears grows loud,
And he knows, now, it's calling him.
He jams down the glass, draws the shade.
The curtains meet, and his comfortable study,
The retreat where he competes with death,
Is again complete about his head.

Five Facets of Myself

I am the twenty-third sermon
Of the learned Jack Donne.
Words and rhetoric funnel me
Through absurdities of conceit.
I am Alice's glass, darkly lit
Like a recess in some movie theater.
I am an ill-conceived Quixote,
Deceiving myself with thoughts
From my outclassed mind.
I swing by my umbilicus
In the cave of Montesinos.

To compete with effete academies
Is like spitting in the Gulf:
No rising tides of insight.
My words, whose insides die,
Are abandoned shells
That no longer hold the roar
Of ancient shores.
Now I am a framed capriccio,
One of Goya's beastly improvisations,
Or a fantastical latter-day saint,
Whose features dissolve in cobwebs
Of Swiftian digression.

My veins burst within the cortex
Of myth and philology.
I gasp for breath.
My poems decay
Like pith in a debarked tree.

Boy of Fits

Who passed through noon's tension,
Its fire-hot wires of boredom?
I did, that day in downtown June.
I melted into the restaurant,
Flowing down quartz-bubbling walks,
Then, seduced by revolving doors,
Was flung into a chorus of single-file,
Sideshow secretaries and nonsectarian
Arcanabiologists.
I did, that Juneloony afternoon.
I ate and spoke with the accidents
Of a liveried world, whose words
Were finely machined and polished
Like insides of a high-compression engine.
I did. I am. I was made privy
Against my whimper, made judge
Of actions, the lord high exchequer
For futile funds and vapid sounds.
I was made to vie with businessmen
And lunch people and lawyers.
I did. I was Benvenuto Houdini
Of my own solitude, playing tricks
With the solar plexus of ambition
And immortality. I was the game,
But Momus held the winning cards.

Confinement

A night too cold for plants:
Palmettos and palms, mangroves
Shiver, ruffling the breeze.
I play solitaire with subtle drafts,
Freezing under Florida blankets.

The cottage winks; its sallow eyes
Blink at the Gulf.
"Poor bastards that live in water,"
I think,
"Sinking under weightless billions.
That I were Vardaman's fish!"

A writer on fire, burning
Under scratchy covers,
Turning out secondhand thoughts
Bought at too high a cost.

Under night,
A slick Brancusi seal,
Alabaster and pumiced soft,
Whiter than Ahab's hatred,
Scurries across my screen.
No easy dream, this one!

A Pierce-Arrow,
Sculpted on someone's rolling mill,
Hurries down endless streets;
Seals and cars retreating fast,
Emblems of freedom and lust
Lost as undiscovered treasure.

Beatrice lives between the legs
Of a too-fast sunrise.
I awaken,
A trembling Dante,
Exiled in a twenty-year yawn.

Election

A blue light,
Through cool, greying night,
Shimmers like eels,
And the ears burn.
Shadows turn in on themselves.
The eyes are learning to see
Through the silence and wet.

An insurgent current
Upstages the mind,
Unwinds the body's thread.
The ebb flows backward —
Life on the verge.
Far out, a fish flips,
Disappears in a grey-blue pool.

Storm: A Dialogue

Spanish thieves in sandaled feet,
Wanting the "secret intelligence,"
Chased sightless beggars down streets
Too dark for common sense.

"Who put the storm out there
To shatter my sleepy rhymes
Like illusions lost to the aging blind
When they find their second sight?"

Angels wearing purple cloaks
Shed raiment and went naked
Through meadows piping poppy fumes,
By lakes with upturned fish.

"Who told rain to fall upward
And wither my thirsty dreams
That grew accidentally perfect
Like hyacinthine verse?"

A one-eyed sailor stood alone
On a beach no map disclosed,
Dashing stones in a mean, hungry sea
That started tides to shake the world.

"Who tucked thunder under the pillow
To muffle my restive sounds
Like waves that ride onto the shore
And hide themselves in shells?"

Nightingales covered with blood
Tottered in tedious, tandem flight,
Casting shadows against red winds
That fought to ruffle their brains.

"Who sent screenrending winds
To scatter my clouded thought
Like birds that waft to limbless trees
In lands they've never seen?"

Children hung with choking faces
And sockets dripping afterbirth
Swung from fast-whirling chandeliers,
Singing poems the silence heard.

"Who threw lightning against the lids
To pock my infant insight
Like bullies hurling burning sand
In eyes of five-year-olds?"

But as I lay beneath the sheets,
The moon broke in the east,
And all my doubts retreated fast,
And I returned to easy sleep.

I saw the thieves in sandaled feet,
That one-eyed sailor on the lee
Leave off the chase, set down the stones,
And pray forgiveness for their deeds.

Nightingales smoothed their ruffled blood,
Flew soft above scudding clouds,
And angels retreated from pagan fields
To don their purple mourning shrouds.

Children hung with choking faces,
Swinging from fast-whirling chandeliers,
Climbed down to wash away the waste,
Singing poems to my tranquil ears.

"Who can cage a dream at work
And insight clouded in infancy
Or restive sounds or sleep-filled rhymes
That fight to free man's poetry?"

Up from Exile

Beatrice was a whore,
The temptress who raised Florence
In a single evening
From a gloomy forest to Paradise.

Her wetness,
An Arno of endless restlessness,
Flooded my eyes,
Where enraptured images
Vied with sterility.

Now, we run after each other
Like ends of a perfect circle.

Dr. Johnson's Rain

I

It's the weather. The legs swell to enormous size.

Another day spent inside a bottle of camphor.
No Happy Valley this hot garret,
Where he meditates entries for a dictionary
And a candle drips drops of immortality
From a flame that festers in his raw-red eyes.

"Father! Father!" he cries. "Why can't I define you?"

He walks into the next afternoon through the fog,
And groggy gloom drips from walls, thatched roofs.
The cobbled water collects in puddles
Beneath his scrubby shoes, and his foot kicks
Imaginary obstacles above the blistered bricks.

"Father! Father!" he sighs. "Why can't I find you?"

An unclean wind thumbs leaves and other debris
Against his haggard face. At his back, the past
Repeats itself in the pitter-pat, pitter-pitter-pat
That saturates lumbering Thames, whose calm
Gives way to the graceful rape of perfect circles.

It's the weather. Hell's dregs flood his eyes.

II

A slovenly figure, fatter than marble statuary,
Goes lonely along Thames' muddy quays.
There are no spectators, no tattlers today
To testify to his silent, dying defiance.

His head is wet under thick rain. Grey stains
Collect like grease on his creased greatcoat,
Melt into motley sameness. Will these blemishes
Go unnoticed by the frail Mrs. Thrale?

"Father! Why didn't I understand your wisdom?

"What the knowledge, the fatuous quotations:
Martial, Livy, Lucan, Pliny the Elder, and Plato.
What easy philosophy! What pedants' canticles
It all was before your quiet, compliant eyes!

"Father! When is penitence consummated in action?

"Those slow eyes on mine, circles on the surface.
Something awakens thoughts of love that, in youth,
Fashioned immortality from a pair of ragged shoes,
And I see you now, seller among vacant bookstalls."

III

"Father! Father! I've been so apart from you.
Let me return to where we started together.

"Oh, Father! For the memory that washes backward
To the simpler, unstudied words and a head
That looks beyond poetry's borrowed ideas.
Let your demise comfort me now and those eyes
Light paths more ancient than Thames' tides!

"Father! Father! How does one as old as I
Do rituals for the mind's forgotten spirit?

"Oh, Father, from whose temple I tumbled too fast,
If it's not been too long coming, then hear me
And accept this hat I hurl to the river's hands,
That I may leave now and need never return
Through this crying rain to Uttoxeter plains."

Caddy's Sin

An abstracted disease,
Ennui,
Creeps,
Lurking in purple shadows,
Where indecision bellows
Helplessly as Benjy.

The Seer

When I look back into the future,
I see history pimping for doges
And brocaded ladies for lesbians.
I hear gimps pounding their gavels,
Eunuchs barking for courtly order,
And revellers quartered in every corner
Of a land gone mad as castrated bulls.

Can't they see those dicing lords
Changing coinage every night
Like prostitutes in temples of the groin?
Won't they heed the feigners and whores
Who lust behind baptistry doors by day,
Pray to alligators and sacred snakes
When night leaves off the panting moon?

Don't they know their future tense
Is but futile hope to regain a past
They chose to ignore in childbirth
Or that the present holds in check
All promises of a graced futurity,
Every immortal expectation,
In a land that has no memory?

When I used to look upon the future,
I saw bystanders no longer innocent,
Whose eyes were shades snapped up
By multiringed fingers of the blind.
Yet who could help see atrocities
Parading each May in ermine mantles
Or babes wrapped in morgue-white shrouds,
Victims of infanticide, genocide,
And extravagant abortionists?

Who could look upon his elders then,
When they hid from themselves
In air-raid shelters beneath the day?
Who would dare say experience
Was the great Socrates of ignorance,
When any little secretary or livery boy
Could toy with immediacy so easily?
Who could see the zealous preachers
When handmaids stole their golden robes?

We bowed, like circus elephants
Consecrating their applauded dance,
When we crowded before altars for praise.
We'd been sufficiently domesticated
To crate ourselves away from one city
To another less harried antipode.
We married (some of us did, anyway),
Only to hide from alien neighbors.
What unfavorable times before the grave!

When I look beyond my present future,
I see something unattainably bright:
Three concentric circles of blinding light
Shimmer like blue-green neon eels.
But the mind buckles like a whiplashed bridge,
And that gap stays closed to my passage
As I float in limbo, consequentially.

Jan's Song

Each March twenty-third

Who can ever know
From words about ideas
Alone
That verbs of finest style
Are formed of feelings
Undisclosed?

Who can say for certain
That words blurted out
Aloud
Don't consist of whisperings
That lie too often
Unaroused?

Who can judge the self
By what it says to
Others,
When only minute trickles
Come back in words
Of silent love?

FIVE

Epiphany

. . . an old . . . horse galloped away in the meadow.
— T. S. Eliot, "Journey of the Magi"

A loud, thick night
Crowded our noisy sleep;
Its soft rain burned window frames
That held no glass.
That world on fire,
Where vertical and flat coalesced
Like colliding stars,
Singed our naked raiment,
Charred infinite half-lives of lust.
And there
In the eastern breach,
Where lightning shadowed the darkling sky,
Was a star too hot to recognize.

And I remember thinking,
"Something is being born
Somewhere."
But her teeth on my tongue
Repeated rituals of joyous strife,
And we grew to ripeness
In that season's brightest moment.

Somewhere, an angel stirred from hiding.
Three palominos,
Halos of Oriental brass,
Each hosting a ghost of an ancient order,
Passed through the burning frames,
Where the glass should have been,
And galloped away in the meadow.

That weary trio,
Decked with ragged panoply —
I had seen them before,
In a less satisfactory life
Perhaps,
Coming by camel or dinosaur,
Had heard their sandaled feet
Beating hard the pavements
In alien village streets,
*

Retreating from hostile calumnies
Into warmer climes reeking with fruit.
But where? When? And who had warned me
They were coming again?

My lips drew out her supple milk
Like hands of a craftsman
Unthreading strands from a tapestry.
"A host-drought consecration," I thought.
And then I knew the pagan ghosts
Come walking, come riding hard
Through deserts marred with crowded life,
Through courts diseased with endless wealth
And patronage and grave intrigue.
"Was I He who died so long ago,
And she, who lay upon my left,
The one who gave immaculately
That gift of matchless ecstasy?"

But she tasted my tongue too harshly,
And the blood ran sharp as salted pap
Where her teeth bit blistering lips.
I had sipped the whiteness of maternity,
But her breasts went dry from my gluttony,
And I cried like an orphaned child
Into the meadows' stifled ears.

The rain no longer spoke to us,
Was kept outside by rattling frames
That held a glossy, foggy glass.
The burning fires sizzled cold,
So the ears could hear no coming hooves,
And the eyes could only see themselves.
We slept like lovers born to die
In ageless acts of infamy.
And the three who had come riding by,
Burning like halos of the sun,
Rode on with gifts of flaming gold,
Into the mangers of the night,
Away in meadows of the sky.

Curse

*. . . him there they found
Squat like a Toad, close at the ear of Eve;
Assaying by his Devilish art to reach
The Organs of her Fancy, . . .*
— John Milton, *Paradise Lost*

I sit on bony haunches,
Smoking a perpetual cigarette
In the shadow-splayed kitchen.
An orange sink light
Mocks my busy silence,
And I await something,
Keeping impatient vigils —
The ritual of midnight hours.

Stillness follows me;
Hollow ticktocks
Fall through blank gravities,
And the refrigerator's whir
Stirs air around my ears.
Now I see her there,
A wandering gypsy, asleep.

She rolls through trances of heat,
A stillborn angel
Whose fingers read
Brass bedposts' ancient braille.
I'm the slinking ghost
Who whispers lascivious thoughts
In her dreaming ears.

Though we've grown like weeds
Filling spaces between nature
And nighttime,
A voice still cries,
"Let me know warm insides,
Where nothing dies and wetness
Grows gardens in the eyes."

There's nothing in that though,
I know,
And a black angel lights on the lids,
Dimming my vision.
*

I feel the curse's weight
Bending my neck to the cave's floor,
Where nothing grows
Save blind, black frogs
And darkness behind the eyes.

Repulsion

She lies there,
Leaking tears that speak
Liquidly as drunken soliloquies,
Repentant and wrong as winter
When buds still cling to bees.

I am the golden apple,
The silver blossom that falls,
Still clawing the writhing,
Soft-spilling belly,
Sinking under twenty centuries of sin.

She sits nude,
A bohemian Eve,
Weightless on bony haunches,
Detesting life that lies
Comfortably between lewd legs.

I, a vengeful Adam,
Bolt from her bedroom,
Half clothed and dank,
Wanting to leave forever,
Knowing severance is impossible.

Expulsion

The eyes' dim light goes dark as beer,
And I hear angels' raucous chants
Dancing in my ears.
   All's gone from this world!
  Tongues droop like dog tails.
  Eyes locked tight as deposit boxes
Hide their contents behind heavy blinks.

Do you remember that first, fast kiss
Or the last purge of youth
In wet bedsheets?
   All's gone from this world,
  Where, once, friends smiled,
  Ran races with each other,
Passing our names like relay batons.

I sing a blind-tired song tonight.
Lightheaded memories leap barren furrows
Where we planted sighs.
   All's gone from this world!
  Mad seeds scattered wild
  About that child/woman's eyes,
But the season was bad for harvesting.

Quick winds split our dust-dry dreams
Against walls built of saber teeth;
We were eaten alive.
   All's gone from this world!
  Two thousand evil years,
  Repeated in a solitary lapse,
Were mastered by bastard importunity.

She's gone from this world of light.
A portion of my mind is lost
In the sea's extremities.
   All's gone from this world!
  I am a blighted Pharaoh,
  Harrowed by another's curse,
Bursting like fish eyes out of water.

Where are you, daughter, when I cry,
"Bring me nosegays to bathe in
When I pray
        (All's gone from this world!),
    Sinless bowers to lie under,
    And a sun too bright to hide behind
When I look for you inside myself"?

The Quick

A touch of summer fills out the night
Like wind in rigging running wing and wing.
Opaline whiskers whisper through trees,
Whose limbs would erase them for the breeze
That sways, stays, whisks them crazily.
Goats pasted against an eccentric sky,
Disguised as satyrs, rape the eyes.
The moon, a bobber on a hungry lake,
Dilates with weight of all this stillness
Down here. Lightning-bug stars
Sear sides of the eyes' horizon,
While a shadow of the man hides, naked,
In its own outreaching across the lawn.
Only a shade of his former self
Retains definition. Age has debarked him;
He is a telephone pole, belfry, a felled cross,
Outraged Ishmael clinging to a coffin
As night reels out to sea,
Liberated for the final inward tug.
There is no other hour except the trees,
The breeze, and random moon. He is a man,
Or haughty silhouette of his past, a sun
Casting shadows that, with every dusk,
With every backward glance, consume him,
Until the moments of his breath coalesce
In that most blessed equanimity, death.

"A HARD COMING OF IT" AND OTHER POEMS
1967

A Hard Coming of It

The Law of God exact he shall fulfil
Both by obedience and by love, though love
Alone fulfil the Law; thy punishment
He shall endure by coming in the Flesh
To a reproachful life and cursed death, . . .
— John Milton, *Paradise Lost*

A stranger in the night
Has come to White Cross
This Christmas of the year.
Undercover agents from Gethsemane
And Olive Branch,
Cities that garrison the fringes,
Press up snugly under shrouds.
Myth and personality coalesce,
Celebrating their annual renaissance.

The man, whose intellect
Spans interstices of history
(He's a twenty-century-a-year man),
Alights from his carre
        (Some say it's a golden sleigh)
And walks into night's silent carnival.

Neons finger his bewhiskered face,
Mistake him for a chaste mannequin.
There's something mystical
About this ubiquitous figure, who sees
Himself
Reflected in every department-store display
As he wends his way,
Unavoidably narcissistic,
Down the city's via media.

It's a potpourri city, White Cross,
Conglomerate of embossed descendants
And easy politico-philosophers,
Musty remnants of Old World stock:
French and Spanish fur trappers,
German brewers and clockmeisters,
Who drifted down De Soto's channels
From more constricted sources of inspiration.

He'll have to see the children
Of marble statuettes, who sit passively
Before daylong TVs and coffee tables.
He must confront broadloom societies,
Ottoman and brocade ladies,
Who parade their boys
And lust-bellied daughters
Like wind-up toys on Florentine chains.

He knows integrity and sophistication,
Unlike names of a brokerage firm,
Enlist no specious supporters
From this atavistic race of moderns.
Were there ever such animals,
These post-Pentateuch creations,
Before Noah's peregrination?

Who could have ever guessed
The only surviving creatures
Would be Ashtoreth's golden calves,
Sperm-grey elephants, and worms
With human faces — abstractions
That fit some middle-class conception
Of itself, a clown's ludicrous shoes?

It's been a long journey,
Reminiscent of some Magi's senseless trek.
He's come with belly flabby
From ballpark "red-hots"
And a hundred and one other elixirs
That sell as phosphates once did
At marble-countered drug stores.
He's come by the city's snoozing limits,
Walking fugitively at the right hand
Of no One, absorbing thorny insults
Under flickering, gaslit penumbras.

Only, there's a task to be performed,
A service to be rendered, this night.
He's a vendor, the maintenance man
*

Who repairs and replenishes machines
When their slots go dry.
He's the artificial inseminator
Who comes once a year
Wearing royal purple faded red by time
And menstrual peculation
(Abortions that confuse creation),
Denied light by the dark flood
And the blood of Mary's little lamb.

As he walks, he spies a light,
A different kind of glow.
It's not the soft yellow of kitchens
Nor passenger cars spanning stretches
Through which he passed in youth
(Duluth, White Cross once, New Haven:
The million and one clichés,
Exclamation points, and dry-plain junctions
Recommended by Rand McNally, Prince Henry . . .
He a kind of embryonic Claus even then)
Nor soft-filtered hallway beams
And bedroom lamps burning early
Over tucked-in heads of fairy children.

No! As he walks alone,
Gathering stray shadows under his feet
Like ten thousand prurient Eves
Gladly accepting defeat or children
Doomed to the piper's mythic lute,
A light
(Some newer kind of helpmate),
Harsh and silverywhite
As a fish's upturned belly,
Jumps out, meets him halfway.

And he thinks as he goes,
Dreaming of sounds and causes
Sourceless and artificially bright,
And he knows that all's gone
From this former world of light.
He imagines himself a secular messiah,
Whose blackened mitre
*

Is nailed to a scarecrow's head,
Whose silver scepter is tarnished
Beyond human recognition.

But he goes ahead along the fence
(Fences are always there,
Pales for stray leaves and newspapers
And subversive notices now;
These white picket mountains
No longer creak under martyred weight)
And by stolid row houses and flats
That slumber complacently
On this preseason Advent.

He speaks to the darkness this eve,
When snow flows like fatted manna
Or wedding rice from well-wishers.
There's a ceremony being performed
Somewhere near this maniacal city,
Swaddled and shivering numbly
In the Mississippi's manger-valley.

He walks on in his own company,
Companionless except for that shadow
Of his female confidante
(Mrs. Claus, as some theologians have it),
Which (Who) lingers like netted memory.
He trudges until Spirit strangles him
And the tumid bag he swings over his shoulder
Like a polar peddler explodes
(Taking twelve months to conceive),
Swallowing him. The morning bursts,
And his breath dies, rather starts anew;
Something is born, breaks its sac.

At once his breath is consumed
In two thousand shouts of glee
And fetid expectancy.
The Christmas pageant slaps his back,
And life starts. (Bosses pass out cigars,
Turkeys, or electric can openers.)
He witnesses the reenactment:
*

Birth old and nascently reformed.
He hears the penetrant rending
Of sacrificial wrappings and ribbons
And stuffings and marrow and wishbones
(Only one at each table gets the heart),

And yet he knows why he's come
All this way for the solitary day
On which they'll rend him
And tear him limb from cedarn limb,
Burn tree-clipped tungsten candles
In effigy, fasten his corona to doors,
And hang his long woolen underwear
From their gaslit hearths:

It's for love alone he's journeyed;
It is love he has carried with him,
A love with which he'll return
To hold in trust
(A form of due bill, some speculate)
Till the children come of age
Or forfeit his day,
Irrevocably.

Essie

A warm woman,
Heart of three girls,
Beating with liquored pulse,
Not reprobate nor lost
But auctioned by quick events
At a ridiculous cost.

Bereft of gold and myrrh,
The wise one still,
Coming slowly over lifeless hills
To this lush Gulf shore,
Planting Cadmusian seeds
To sprout and revenge herself
With images of Saint George.

Esther from the Garden,
Her kerchief soiled yet white
As life-germ, ranges wide
To Calvary's summit.
The seeds of ancient Mordecai
Thrive on her energy.

Minor immortality:
Life that grows above the ground.
Outside, a coldblack night
Wrinkles wet as eels.
An albatross drops from her neck,
Throwing off wingspray
Against the eyes' newer night,
And she submits to sleep,
Counting sheep that pass in threes
Beneath her tired lids.

Heading North from Friday

Friday afternoon.
A red-pregnant circus sun,
Balloonhung and burning slow,
Turns across the sky's tongue.
Now, molting hues
Bluegold to pewter,
Friday roars, mute
As lion cubs,
Through dusk's fuzzy cage.

A day gone blind,
Drawing behind its ebb,
Like shore-receding waters,
Myriad suggestions of Calypso.
A car too silver for night
Digresses in shadowed retreat,
Pulling its squeal behind it.

We drive on together,
Past fastrushing lawns,
By lackluster farms and pastures
Wombed with picket fences.
Highway 67,
A quick, Egyptian god,
A Nile gone hard,
Stretching orthodoxly
Over unleavened Illinois soil.

We drive on, into darkness.
Lambent eyes cast insults,
Despising our naked speed,
Our uterine security,
And the uneasy freedom
That exists in the motion of things.

"Where are you from?"
Someone once asked us.
"Anywhere," she replied.
Now she sighs,
Sinking into sleep's vibrations,
Thinking aloud,
"Where are we going now?"
*

"Somewhere north from today,"
I say,
Trying to keep night
Before my orient eyes.

Unmatched Ecstasy

They thrive by the score,
Living without growing
Under a folded roof,
In houses painted with juicy steaks
And occult spoofs on nomenclature.
Beneath stapled impermanence,
Martinets with red helmets
Stand at static attention.
Frequent visitors open their door,
Snap them one at a time,
As hunters winter cornstalks.
But they crave fresh air,
And the rasping flick
Down runways
Flecked with skid marks
Sets the halo flying.
A glow guides the curling body,
Until a shudder chokes it white.
Then each knows, in that instant
Before it lies discarded
In table graves,
In front-yard gutters,
The glory of its painless death.

Student Prince

For Jan,
in April

I

He sits on a sofa
In some ocean-soiled apartment,
Head against the wall,
Not realizing his two lit cigarettes
Burn in tandem.

The sandaled feet
Twitch like galvanized muscles
On the table before him
As he thinks of culture
And Christ mounting Calvary;
He's a religious bastard,
Even in despondency.

It's a late afternoon,
Soiled as dirty lingerie.
The hours parade like grey rhinos,
And rain slithers down drainpipes,
Washing the day's green dust
From mangroves and royal palms.

He hears shouts and tired voices
Retreating in twos from the beach.
Cycles churn ceaseless vibratos,
Burning down A1A,
While drug-injected throats
Of four hundred horses
Roar importunately
Above the rain's soft tappets.

Cars, like Moses' miraculous wand,
Part slippery streets
Outside, beneath his window,
Throwing off sounds
The color of yellow nausea.
His ears grow sullen and wince.
The eyes see lightning
About the lamp's frayed cord;
*

Sparks of clear, jagged skies
Ricochet against shadowy baseboards,
And all is aglow,
Momentarily.

But he just sits,
Shivering from too much burn,
His curly hair
Turning a thousand twirls
At wrong angles.
He's silent as a windless winter
In this summering spot,
Where hot-puckering suns wizen skin
Until fingers and forehead
Become mummies out of gauze.

II

He's spent the day
The way the children do it,
Prostrate against the sand.
He's seen the unpurged bodies
Of good-looking college kids,
All of them grown riotous
As shades in Hell,
Each an athlete in motel rooms,
Porky's bar,
Or the car's backseat at night.

It's one great revival here,
Where he's come to preach the gospel.
He's traveled by thumb and car
To drool over bikinied flesh
And meet the wise men
With guitars and adolescent poetry
That drips like saliva
Off demotic tongues.

But he's forgotten his words,
Left them at Crazy Greg's
Or somewhere else along the "wall."
He can't compete with screeching gulls,
*

Radios' dull cacophonies,
Or the ocean's predictable swell.
Perhaps it's all just as well.

III

He wants to smoke both cigarettes;
His stomach muscles strain
As he brings lips into filtered heat.
The painful, burning bite of nicotine
Eats his eyes, and he thinks of culture
And the gifts and juvenescence.

Those gifts placed at his feet,
Veronica's kerchief,
And tears the ground-dust drank
Before he could stoop, could touch,
All float to the mind's ceiling
Like balloons released by accident.
The hot-awful pinpricks
Through the wrists and ankles,
The visceral slit leaking grapefruit
For lack of caustic unguents
Still pain his writhing thoughts,
Thoughts that run wild as lunatics
Over his tongue's vindictive lawn.

"You bastards behind the tans.
That I were a forever man,
Able to wander these fabled coasts
With leopard spots for freckles,
Eating the pard's liver for strength!

"That I could change like serpents
And rend these purple robes
That rub the raw, red waist
With each dry molting!
Then you'd see me as I am:
Just another of your kind,
Wearing madras trunks, Coppertone,
And maybe a shark's tooth about my neck
Or a surfer's Croix de Guerre.

"That I were reptilian,
Groveling in zoo pits, aquariums,
An alligator writhing wildly
Through endless daytime shadows,
With eyes pulled down like shades
Against prying, paying tourists,
An alligator whose body grows
An inch at a time
From Easter to Easter.
Then,
When rain pelted the scaly back,
I'd live atop my friends,
Brothers of the slime,
Reptiles of sunless dens.

"But tonight I'll drink beer
Without thoughts of charity
And works that spill like dross
From your preachers' unflossed cavities.
And tomorrow . . . tomorrow, I'll have coffee
With parched toast or buttered muffin,
Then take off again,
Wearing buffalo sandals,
Carrying this wrinkled staff
Over my shoulder.

"I'll walk the beach,
And there, where the water ends
And land resumes
And each knows each other
As of the same species,
I'll crawl up slowly,
Open wide my jaws,
And slither fast into the underbrush,
Flapping my tail behind me."

Boats Against the Current

Day-before-yesterday snobberies
Suggest refuse
(Dung heaps,
Garbage steeped in all-black
Backyards);
They rest anachronistically
As Whitehall chain mail.

Who ever knows what "fixings"
Rode wings of meretriciousness
Or who the "solid" party was
To unreal shenanigans
Washed clean by fanatical few,
Who rushed to ticket booths
To claim "accidental" quinellas?

The Wolfsheims, Esteses, Bakers:
Yesterday's urchins bookmakers
Admired and feared,
Their sons elevator jockeys,
Delivery boys chauffeuring corsages
To LaDue parvenus.

But the refuse, slime,
From which climb the Gatz-bys,
Lady Ashleys . . .
Isn't it primogenial
And sound, too, the slime
That windfalls and landfalls
Bulldoze,
Then refill with newer men?

Can't you see them,
The ruptures,
Dike fissures, everywhere
In a world patently corrupt?
Don't you realize they're unseen
At first? They come slow,
Then burst like flourishing Judas trees.

The trouble doesn't rest with the people
Necessarily
Nor in the dreaming either
*

But with what they leave behind
In wakes of hurried tradition —
I mean the others,
Those wide-jawed dreamers,
Those hind-duggers drinking dust
And ignored by select success.

I accept my station
Gracefully,
Though I'd gladly submit
To mobile poverty
If some understanding economist
Could teach me to exchange
My ninety-dollar suit
For bushels of wheat
Or mattocks to dig Indians
And pigtailed blacks
From embryonic graves.

But don't you see?
It's that the dream,
The possibility, does exist,
Breeds like mosquitoes
On the eye's swollen surface.

Yet,
That the dream persists,
Lepidopteral, unreal,
Is, at best, tentative.
Don't you see?
Can't you see this?

For who can tell tomorrow's children
That today's milkman
Was yesterday's lawyer's son,
That their benefactors
Were dentists a decade before,
Or that one fine day
Their own offspring
Might be Israeli kings
Or buried under slime
In Thessaly?

Loomings

The day breathed grey
And cold-dark sighs at dawn.
It lay heavy
Over our house,
Like an opaque paperweight
Atop fliers and bills
Or a hoot owl's plaint
Gone silent over a busy forest.
I walked outside
To breathe the quick, crisp dawn,
Gliding with its insomniac strides,
Then felt a sudden urge to go inside.

Inquiring Adam

. . . be lowly wise:
Think only what concerns thee and thy being;
Dream not of other Worlds, what Creatures there
Live, in what state, condition or degree, . . .
Raphael, VIII, 173–176

But apt the Mind or Fancy is to rove
Uncheckt, and of her roving is no end; . . .
Adam, VIII, 188–189

— John Milton, *Paradise Lost*

Someday,
When unicorns
Drip in single file
From the kitchen spout
And drop,
Nimble as lions
On all fours,
Onto the porcelain sink,
I'll pause on the brink
Of discovery
And shout,
"Raphael,
            I
      Disagree!"

The Withheld Sensibility

Whoever mothered mildwild bugs
That leak nightlight
In the mind's whitewet palm,

Whoever ran fast through larch
Or matted juniper at dusk,
Chasing a shadow of former love,

Must confess
Life's unrecoverable beauty
To himself,

Just as the bent
Narcissus
Spoke the meaning
Of Benjy's deeper moaning
For him.

Ritual

I never knew youth
Could last so long,

Then explode
In
Freedoms of female entanglement.

Silent fire burning off,
Consuming accumulated desire;
Sun eating morning frost
From selfish lawns . . .

Somewhere, a weary angel stirs;

I emerge.

A Fourth of July rocket
Sears the eye's horizon
Tonight:

A celebration of the seasons,
The personal creation.

Small breasts grow in palms
Moist with loving.

An angel stirs.

Stray beams skitter through venetian-blind teeth,
Screaming down fine, private walls
Of this ancient confessional.

A rite is being performed;
An urgent current flows through us:
Some haughty Thames
Or floodclogged
Zürichsee.

Will we ever return to ourselves?

The Hunters and the Hunted

I

I walk out alone this morning,
Before the traffic,
Bent with singular intention,
Rattles my madness
With importunate drones.

As I walk the green and pied fields
Of briar and winter wheat,
A sweetcold scent of onion
Whispers through the nostrils.

I step staccato, stalking rabbits,
Tripping over groundvines
That line intricate runs
Smooth as a bird's nest's belly.

Walking alone,
Shotgun draped like cloth
Across the weary arm,
I think how she waits,
Contemplating my solitude.

II

Done now; the car rushes back
Through pewter sunsets
Toward distant White Cross.
The stomach gurgles like floodwater,
Feeding impatiently on itself.

Nighttime, and I think
How I walked the fields this morning,
How alone out there
Without her.
Now all is changed.
There are no creatures to hunt.

III

A naked creature crouches,
Eve of some ancient conception,
Shoots wild,
Writhing into subtle fruit.

Skin folds into skin,
And somewhere an angel stirs,
Delivering us from ourselves.
She is outright giving
The gift reserved for once and only.

The eyes fill moist;
The lips go dry, slightly foxed —
Paradox of the seasons.
Rain settles in remote regions,
Spraying the mind's garden.
Something is being born.

IV

I know the spine's subtle curvature,
The "I love you," simply spoken,
Inadequate token of the world's religion.
We rest between generations,
Ten thousand voids coming open.

We are among the martyred handful,
Profligates of our own invention,
Toppling Pilate's cedar trees
Like Cyclopes dashing rocks.

We are the human animals
Lured out of coiled hissing,
Silent as seeds
Twitching under soil's first tillage,
Awaiting resurrection.

Suggestions of Demise in an Occasional Professor of Modern Poetry

His trouser-baggy legs
Are trees lost in a forest
Of insidious undergrowth;
His shoes' dyspeptic laces
Snakes that dangle from twigs
In a jungle of raceless natives.
Those knees that trunk the paunch
Buckle with each dramatic strut
As he reflects, through words
That genuflect like Indians
Before Coronado's dreams of wealth,
Colossal thoughts of impossible schemes.

His splotchy hands tear the air
Before his gnarled face; his hair
Shares spaces with tangled sounds,
And he cackles, bellows, grunts,
But reverberations of ancient drums
Free tympana of conundrums
He no longer needs to explicate.
A smile, a somber, parading cortège,
Traces across his facial horizon.
His thoughts range like minute water striders
Chasing diminishing circles they make.
Though notions of change and death
Etch no poems on his rubbery ears,
He clears his throat to expatiate
And, with clichéd coda, disappears.

Keep the Fires Burning

For Larry Cartwright

Who can hear the silent pine
Whining,
Bereaving a boy's departure,
Or the soft-trod paths
Pumiced under no boy's feet?
Will the Wisconsin breeze
That settled in summering ears
Breathe in a boy's newer dreams
In some unforgetting bed?

I know the secret of everything!
It's friends, boys!
It wends through the spruce
And folds beneath waters;
It sits at your table
And hides beneath your pillow.

Who can refuse that gift,
The harbinger that comes calling
Like a happy beggar
Behind parting farewells
And when snow and rain
Detain the slower spirit?

I am witness to summer's grace.
You are the ones, boys!
This is the place!
Don't be forgetting
Nor ever regretting the myth
That is your birth,
For being born comes fast,
Sometimes;
It matures in the youngest mind,
Sometimes.

Boys! Boys! This is the truth!
How can you not know?
Growth is that sacred moment
When all else falls away
And all that stays
*

To remind you it ever was
(The growing)
Is the faith that those
Who breathed and slept,
That those who ate and played
With you, tomorrow's men,
Will always be your mates
When you say the words
"Friend"
And, again,
"You are my friend!"

Cottage by the Gulf

The strip of beach
Filled up with loose-billed sounds
Of sandpipers, gulls, and pelicans.
Our cottage was Venice,
Mounted on ancient staves
Above the sandy tides.

We sat on the porch,
Watching the Gulf gather speed.
Waves, like a palm's windy fronds,
Uncurled onto the shore,
While its windscorched lips,
As if in pantomime,
Absorbed smaller oceans of spray,
One at a time.

We gazed out silently
Behind the violent monster,
This gargantuan sea.
Far out,
Beyond a swelling forest of breakers,
A baleful gardener
Walked atop waves, raking their crests.

I sighed. She balked with fright,
Ran into the cottage to hide.
"Something's not right!" she cried.
"This is a slutty Gulf!" I shouted.
"A real prostitute!
You can't ever predict
When it'll seduce the weather."

I watched the sky
Fill up with vapour
As far as the eye could detect.
Soon, the wind shifted directions,
And the cottage, a web
Stitched loosely to decaying twigs,
Lifted once but held secure.
Then I was sure I knew
The grating whine that frothed
And barked at the darkening sky.
"Hurricane!" I cried,
As I ran inside to pray.

Selma, Alabama, 3/6/65

For Wendell Rivers

Racist, Jew, fanatic, gentile,
Apologist, Southerner, Anglophile —
I am all these things today,
Things that curse, things that pray,
Things that don't know what to say
Or think or dream. My mind kneels
In dusty roads. My knees know fatigue,
And I can't even whimper.

I want to vote, like other things
That qualify as human beings.
I tell myself that I'm a man.
I face the lies of democracy,
Am singed by its senseless fires.
I cry sometimes in my separate room,
Where birth and death are inseparable
And equal, but they do not heed
What I need to say and dream and do.
They claim that *be* and *seem*
Are not the same, that *ought*
And *should* could only be bought
At a cost they'd never pay.

But we'll meet at the church,
Where the road joins a birch copse,
Half a mile from town.
We'll wear our brown skin,
Our black skin, inside out
And ignore their shouts,
For to fight back would be wrong,
Would make us part of the throng
Of innocent ignorance
That preys behind every tree.
We can't submit to the hordes
That disgrace themselves,
Knowing they sow scornful seeds
In the soil of all men's dignity.

We'll march while the sun's in hiding,
Start running as it rises to shadows.
What other way is there to say
That we're not just fractional things,
Unless all men be puppeteers'
String-moved slaves?

Let's march now. Let's run now.
I don't know how to whimper anymore.
Let us bow and pray,
Then walk, march, run that race
With the sun. We'll arise today
From three centuries of disgrace
To soothe the sweaty brows
Of children who'll take these vows.

Exigencies

He sits atop parapets
Of the school's museum of art,
Thumping a cigarette
Whose grey ashes
Jump walls of April space.

A radio splatters silence
Nearby,
And his eyes spring spiteful
As maddened cobras;
The ears bite each other.

His mind, a butcher knife on butter,
Splits particles of dust,
And he lapses,
Hardening inside gauzy riddles
Like fortunes in Oriental cookies.

Now he thinks of that cave,
The reason Christ chose to escape:
"What in hell was there
In there
That pared His nerves
Like manicure scissors to nails?

"Was it the darkness,
Nullity
(Our Father, who art in darkness,
Hallow be Thy shallow grave,
Thy cave),
Or was it reverberations
Of His gushing blood
That drove Him from us to Him?"

But it's late, and he should leave
These debates to concentrate
On more immediate things:
Titian and the Greek.
He must memorize discreet answers
The teacher expects to read
On tomorrow's blue-book sheets.

The break over, and he retreats
To hide his head in picture books.
He'll have to study long tonight
And eat from vending machines.
"The 'complete man,'" he tells himself,
"Is he who learns his lessons well
And leaves abstractions to the poets."

Hobo

They recorded his birth
In a small western town,
Where a nameless father
Gave him his nomenclature.

And he seemed waiting,
Even then,
To flag the trains
That took on baggage and grain.

He became a drummer,
Bumming the freights
That passed day and nighttime,
All hours of summer.

Destinationless,
A ragged outcast,
He was Colorado Nation,
Man of means,
Speculator in soybeans and cabbage,
Mastermind of the great white ways,
A Vegas flunky,
Whose pockets were filled with
                                    grace.

And he ran the pavements,
Denver, Frisco, Spokane,
Even in winter, when rain and sleet
Beat against his brain,
Always retreating,
Always in lewd heat,
Ever seeking a
                    mother.

Once, he died in April,
Just thirty-three,
On an eastbound freight,
In a green, unharvested year,
Frustrated in motion,
Prostrate and bleeding
On the hard cedar floor
Of a Great Western boxcar.

Designs in Storm Time

The sticky Illinois highway
Stretched like tape
Over down-cowed fields.
It was morning, late,
And a greypurple sky
Leered with squint eyes.
Then a sign caught my gaze:
GET RIGHT WITH GOD.
Corn, droopeared as nuns
Retreating in prayer,
Waved me on.

Rain's footfalls
Danced across my roof,
And I watched the morning
Turn from dust to mud.
Lightning, like a scoop's jaws,
Ate the pavement
Fifty yards ahead,
And I coasted into silence.
Wires contracted,
Snapped to the ground,
Glowing white as halos.

Then,
Turning to look behind,
I saw another bolt
Whiplash that listing sign,
Shattering it into charred bones.
"Someone or something menacing
Has trained vengeance
Upon that sacred design,"
I said to myself.
GET GOD WITH RIGHT
Read the electrocuted slogan.

Then a third blast
Juggled the frightened earth,
And I drove away
Fast,
Not being a person
To tempt providence with delay.

The Gathering In: March Ides

A mid-March sun
Breaks out of the ridge of a homespun sky,
Hovers atop a kelp-oak
That could as easily be slippery growth
Swaying with tides beneath the sea.
The tree's steepled twigs glow with fire
No breeze kindles, forming a star
Whose apex grazes the sun's escutcheon.
Is this oak or belated sign of Christmas,
Fastidiously lined with ornaments,
Seeds clustered by natural design?

A huge pupil in the sky's socket
Dilates like a moon come back disguised,
Then dissolves for the grey-quilt clouds.
March wans in its seminal hours.
Ragged tentacles pry denser shards,
Parting the hazy carapace once more
Before swarming to surfaces it forms.
Air the turf releases goes warm,
Then cold with the gradual closing in.
Finger-paint patterns conceal thoughts,
Reveal yellow emotion in secret grooves,
While a migrant thread of blue
Scurries to elude the ubiquitous rift.

Soon, all is quiet, as if night,
Somehow ranging off its seasoned axis,
Has bloomed, relaxing its hold over day.
A greyer light than any before
Proceeds from the source of all that grows
And dies. The mosaic collapses,
Showering debris and pieces of glass
Against the fetid retina. A frustrated sun
Cowers behind saturnine lids.
Trees are blown. The hours groan heavily
As drops clinging to a running spout.
A lascivious snow slithers through pores
Before mating with the accosted earth.

A Wintering Mimosa

The old mimosa, planted out back
In the yard I scavenged as a boy,
Lifts arthritic, splintering bones.
The accomplishing winter whistles
Through its bristled ears,
But it hears no birds noising about
On limbs secured by tarnished wires.
Its blacksmith back leans tediously
Over the turf's unheated anvil.
Each branch, a brittle hammer,
Beats no shape from the icy earth.
Down the side lightning once struck,
Its naked spine shows tarred cankers,
Unnatural bark that exposes its death.

Is this a male or utterly female tree,
Whose molted plumage deceives the eye?
What avatar is this in seasoned disguise,
Whose autumnal phase, like west-drained hues,
Has evolved from shortening days of June
Into shadowy perpetuity?
This *is* night. No ordinary specters roam.
Winter's blight is cemetery grey.
Raw is the ridge where unthawed sod
Bites this icon of prickly life,
Whose blood is sap, whose tissues pods
Disseminated as scattered bones,
Whose trunk is a useless crucifixion —
A body lying upright against the sky.

If an actress poised on her knoll,
She might be a legacy of antique Troy,
A relic of Hector's unheeded affection,
Or an ancestor of Southern belles,
The queen of New Orleans coppices,
That genteel pride of Richmond verandas
And patioed lawns near Charlottesville,
Untouched by greedy, moss-cloyed hands.
Now, a distaff mourner out of party gown,
Frozen at the head of a circular stair,
Sharing her pride with the deadening air,
She patiently awaits no lover's return.

I planted this seed of woman and man
In springtimes of youthful harmony,
Communed through green years of piety,
And carried our love, this double marriage,
Above and beyond the unspoken vows
That set the self outside its house.
But the hours have crowded out the blood,
And I must set my stores in order
Before their fruit gives back my seed —
This tree has grown old inside of me.

The Abiding

Boxwoods and lesser bushes
That buttress this house
Wear extravagant coronas of white.
The house is lost for a night
Just splitting shadowy prisms
I walk through to meet the sun,
Coming out of nothing into day.
Stray starlings and jays
Connect invisible threads
From soft pine to oak
That line morning's perimeters.
I smoke. My vapours coalesce
With freeze the March air breathes.
My breath pushes outward,
Endlessly clear, without rising,
Along a path at odds with the sun.
The feet move easily across lawns
Brittle yet with tight moisture,
Forming runs no rabbits make.
Beyond the fence, the neighbour's pond
Respires — something is warmer than day.
Water's skin wrinkles with first light
The sun raises cautiously above woods
That border his pond, and I see red
Enlarging like microscopic spores
In the pond's circumscribed eye.
A squirrel eludes its fear,
Traces a line, from hutch to hiding,
The breadth of the yard I scan.
Overhead, in its own domain,
A crow shreds the air's wrappings,
Lights preemptorily in the comb
Of a naked oak behind my sight.
The sun, caught in its act,
Is wrapped in smog that congregates
Farther east than Old Man.
My eyes belch, scanning themselves
In that pond, which no longer nets
What minutes before was a Ping-Pong ball
Painted the color of boiled lobster.
*

Something is changed, and now the eyes
Find no counterpoint for the searing.
The ground still takes my weight,
But the feet share its property
With sweet-gum seeds, whose spines
Lie dormant as foetal porcupines.
And here and there, mimosa pods,
Like weathered gondolas,
Mustard-brindled and almost innocent,
Too brittle to be disturbed,
Manage this Adriatic turf,
Set impermanently in gradually uncurling waves
I also walk upon this early.

Already that mass is moving away
From the woods, up from the pond,
And now my breath stays fixed
Inside the nostrils, the feet
Retrace where no runs glisten,
And the ears, unavoidably open,
Listen to the highway's dry-point burin
Scratching persistent burrs
From stertorous wheels over concrete.
On the street beyond my lawn,
A snake slithers toward the cemetery.

A different kind of light glows now.
Trees are merely trees against an earth;
A whitening sky a day that will take
Itself too seriously. And I retreat,
Wondering why people sleep through change
Into less subdued phases of day,
Which we've made for them this dawning.

The Strangler

Pondering the Boston Strangler's
escape from Walpole State Prison,
2/24/67

The neck swells with congestion.
Suggestions of contagion
Are rife in my neighbourhood.
Who would dare deliver milk,
Mail, merchandise from boutiques,
When madmen crawl into keyholes?
Innocence has been threatened
When men confined for life
Vault over neglected scaffolds
Into the snowed-in outside night.
Conventional locks and brass chains
Can't contain inner sanctums
Nor restrain stray perversities
From defiling domestic ovens.

Inquiry into the daring escape
Stops where snow prints
Walk out of themselves into freedom.
A camera pans the abandoned cell;
We see its interior,
Smell the anxious sheets,
Guess at schemes conceived
With the help of the gods.
Behind the myna mouth, mirrored
By a million silvery electrons,
Ticker tapes beat themselves to death,
Competing with this modern Tiresias
For the last say before "sign-off."
The divining rod points toward itself.

We lie in bed in this sheltered flat,
Propped up against a late movie.
Trollies clatter past a stalled car.
Again, the camera, a different eye,
Itches itself into artistic focus
As an obvious actor backs into day.
His riddled Packard goes forward
Of its own accord, conveys his crime
*

Through crowded streets like ink
Invisible under nonviolet beams.
An airplane multiplies his getaway road;
The car runs off the screen,
Into a commercial for better vision.
Suspense is haply interrupted.

Soon the motorcycle has its prey.
We slide deeper into the sheets,
Predicting the inevitable justice
We've seen a thousand times before.
The verdict has only to wait out
Three more intervening commercials,
And the process defines itself.
It's the public threat that matters,
Not the twenty-six dollars
He stole from the fastidious tailor.

Capital punishment is none too good.
But it's an older movie, we know;
Things were different before Freud
Slipped unnoticed onto grocery shelves
And off tongues of dumb attorneys.
Today, we label them insane;
They get put away for behaviour
Deemed psychotically disapprobatory.
It's only the humane, democratic way.

She sleeps, now, while I fidget,
Listening to the wind's thin fingers
Rapping out codes on our window.
Her slow breathing is the wind.
Her dreams leak out before my eyes.
I am witness to her secrets.
My ears tap her fragile wires,
And I listen to those busy signals
That torture her uncolored patience.
A man steps tentatively over wires
She reels out like spider silk
From her cell. He climbs scaffolding
That lines her lidded eyes, descends
*

Onto our snowlike sheets, disappears.
Something is liberated. She contorts,
Springs erect as a cautious cat,
Grabs my insomniac sensibility for comfort.

I know her nightmare before she gasps.
Inquiry comes hard for her.
"It's of no import," I say, though now
I know freedom has no quarters
Where fear feeds itself on doubt.
Somewhere on the street below, a shout
Breaks into day; night gives way
To the clatter of milk bottles.
A truck roars quietly, vomiting its package
Against our ground-floor door.
"Her new dress," I think. A paper waits
In its place. Coffee bolsters apprehension,
Makes headlines bearable. Bold, black print
Strangles the escaped victim, splays him
Comfortingly across the nation's forehead.
Our locks and brass chain have held again.

Shall Rise Again

Owls mourn valleys bullets shred.
Life hovers over dead memories
That have painted dusks red
Every evening since Appomattox
Shed its twin flags. An empress
In her last solstitial phase,
The moon, scimitar out of scabbard,
Whispers a cry before upstaging day.

Another Mother

For Essie

When the last granules scratch the glass neck,
A man will dig more buckets of sand
From islands on which he's stranded himself
And hope to extend his amnesty.
But he stands a slave to his waning age.

Alone in his own failing quietude,
A man will go an untried way
To hear his dry voice echoing
On the farther side of an alien cave.
But his words are gaunt and emasculate.

With his attitude planted before the grave,
A man will pry open his iron lids,
Draw back the tomb's grey-wrinkled face,
Which hides ripe secrets buried in youth,
And cry for that woman who breathed his birth.

When wreaths are hung about his eyes,
A man will lock all his doors for sleep
And creep back into his childhood bunk,
Waiting for his mother to tuck him in
And lie beside him while he says his prayers.

Reductio ad absurdum

Brown brows that should be grey
Grow shrubbery in shades of tired eyes.
Gold rimmed around thick glass
Glistens like two suns in eclipse,
While this ten-year-too-old mind
Defines events emotionally,
Lacking substance that lacks definition.

To his right, a student cringes,
Watching his wrist watch for futurity
That comes regularly each six o'clock
Every Tuesday evening. Academics
Play some sort of mental havoc
With considerations of time
That line his mind with sandbags.

His wrist piece is a neon eye
With ten years' experience
Behind its foreign mind, a brain
Blinking through silent revolutions,
Sprung, cased, and counterbalanced
With metallic precision, guaranteed
To define time, substantially.

Eyes are eyes that underlie memory
Beneath glass that separates the now
From its ever-present recession.
But each (the eyes), when left untended,
Goes predictably slower and slow,
Until lies shatter them and they die,
Each six o'clock, every generation.

Prince of Cigarettes

He's a pastime man,
Whose Class A hobby
Is making tinfoil globes
From cigarette wrappers.
Every carton builds a world,
And when it gets too large,
The garbage collector
Carts it away with napkins,
Corned-beef scraps,
And pulpless orange rinds
That find their way
To furnaces in basement graves.

But who minds being God
Every week or so, even if cancer
Leaks through yellowing lungs?
"That's the price you pay,"
He tells himself,
"When making mountains
Out of charcoal filters,
Silvery Bastilles
From fanatical wrappers,
And ashen molehills
To be buried beneath
When you get too old to contemplate."

Legacy

The son of Fitz-Patrick
Was,
Of necessity, a bastard.
At least,
That's how the word
From above
                    has it,
Etymologically.

Exalted Thought

There's something about singing
That lifts a lowslung spirit;
It's the song sung with soul
That builds the heart,
Fills the whole, slow earth
With a breath
That never forgets its birth.

Narcissus

Not for love nor money but from necessity,
I left the Gulf beach's retreat
To enter these gates, where shades
Masked in human decay breathe out their days
A decade at a time. Here is no paradox:
Suns of antique days barely part live oaks
And ponderous royals and Washingtonias
That line pavements in this warmer clime.
De León might have foreseen inevitabilities
When his fountain refused nourishment
To his scruffy Old World life-stock.

In the park, people that might be leaves
Crinkled and wrinkled, blindly strewn
About benches painted green and lawns
Matted yellow where green was sown,
Listen, like slaves overhearing spectators
In some Academia gallery, to the symphony
Punctually glued to the bandstand's crescent.

I pass through, circumventing feet
Knitted with blue ruptures and tumid faces
Confronting what their ears don't recall
From times foreign to this immediacy.
Even the heavy tuba and bassoon,
The barrel-chested kettledrums' revelries
Wake no signs of recognition in the man
Planted like a desert bush in his lawn chair.
His hands manage a palsied accompaniment.
He leans through twenty bars of "The Mountain King,"
Then resumes his paperback investigations.
Unobtrusively, I pass on toward the other side,
Detected by none save a grinning face
That tilts behind some chronic idiocy,
Spectral prophet of unnatural causes.

The music slithers into air pockets,
Currency that counts in waning decibels,
As I edge slowly away down streets
Parallel to themselves endlessly. The shops here
Are different: jewelry from Faulknerian estates,
*

Antiques, monogrammed pocket watches,
Cameo pendants, diamonds defying credibility;
Gift shops offering plastic fruit in boxes
Under taut cellophane; import stores
Huddled in walls like beggars in Mecca streets,
Displaying ivory icons, Buddhas made in Spain,
Inlaid-pearl music boxes, woven rugs, tapestries
That took someone seven years to weave, a day
To barter for passports and field rifles.

But still I walk, having not yet arrived
At what I came to take back with me.
The streetlight changes, discharging shot,
Each related, every one a vestigial species,
Freaks of ectomorphic distortion.
An ambulance stalls the turgid crowd,
Suspending suspension, and in this moment,
Each face glowers, suspecting itself
Behind those urgent curtains. Now unstalled,
We follow out our trajectory to the other corner.
No one here erects monuments to progress.

Just up the street, the most unique drugstore,
Remnant of defunct petroleum fields, looms:
City within a sprawling community,
Entirely self-contained in callous ubiquity.
Inside, I vie with motherhood. Who would guess
The womb could be this crowded after birth?
But the hothouse blasts its creatures
With preternatural heat. Petals droop,
Leaves parch blacker than untended toast,
And Southern widowhood boasts longevity
Attended by grandfather clocks with canes.
Regulated animation is controlled from above
By the conspicuous nature of vain desires.

I pass through the gates, and faces graze me
Importunately — logs conveyed upstream
To planing mills, whose saws buzz circularly,
Cutting the horizontal cambium from wizened timber
And gnarled cypresses strangled by their roots.
*

I share spasmodic shoving to exist,
Resisting temptations to easy impatience.
I have come all this way from necessity,
To acquire something with which to return.
My mind refills its dwindling catalogue.
I am up for sale. Everything is on display,
From white elephants to chartreuse carnations.
But who can tell, among the tinsel litter,
Where they've stowed my operating equipment?

On the ground level, escalators creak continually.
I opt for horizontality, stop to see grey people,
Prematurely dead, who eat ice cream from boredom;
These children without children of their own
Are too old for carnal pleasures, too adolescent
To regard carnivals and puddles they leave on vests
And bespattered spectacles. Popcorn odors
Eat the air, profaning their personalities,
And perfume leaks from sample decanters
On counters where "crackers" and pygmy tourists
Press tight into newer skins that don't fit either.

Along one corridor, outmoded guidebooks
Reassure accidental Diderots and natives
That exotic plants, trees, deep-sea fishes
From prehistoric categories still exist.
Offset shells fill books with Linnaean completeness,
And I read just enough to know that life
Lies somewhere else than on this shelf
Gathering dust and violate fingerprints.

Upstairs, Tussaud mermaids brood over treasure
In cardboard boxes, their neon breasts
Titillating no one but themselves. There, ransom
Is fit for defunct kings and fatted queens
Out for vacuum cleaners and pillow slips.
My eyes decline, and I explore the bookstore,
Lingering over rows of fairy tales, myths,
And fables from a more favorable time than ours.

One floor above, a pasteboard farmscape,
Set off like a rural fair with crepe and flags,
*

Draws spectators with sensational slogans:
SEE THE BANTY RUTH PLAY BASEBALL . . .
FOR A DIME, YOU CAN WATCH THE LIVE ROOSTER
DO A SCOTTISH JIG . . . FOR ONE THIN DIME . . .
PRIZE HEN WALKS THE TIGHTROPE, SHOOTS BASKETS . . .
FARMER WEBBER'S FANTASTICAL FAIRGROUND FOWLS.

My pockets yield to curious fingers, change jingles,
And I hold up a silvery disk that glints off eyes
Behind the mesh before I slide it down channels
That might be connected to the rooster's pituitary.
Lights belch, reaching toward threshold intensity,
And the door that barred his conditioning from play
Swings open. Electric talons click and scratch
Upon waxed surfaces green as ballpark turf.
A beak pecks tentatively. The wooden bat balks,
Swats a Ping-Pong ball, wafting it three feet
To the sensitized bleachers. . . . Home run!

Lights appear by each base. The fowl prances
As though his trainer were pacing behind with butcher knife.
As he passes each pasted goal, the lights flicker.
The animal dashes down homestretch, importunately.
No teammates greet him. Only pebbly grits,
Feed, pelt tinnily inside the cage's container.
A beggar rushes in, pecks grain the machine vomits,
Then settles into prolonged insatiety
For the next entrepreneur with a silver coin.

I rush to escape children tied to balloons
That float like cartoon captions behind them.
Where is it? Why does a person such as me
Have to search among relics, antiquated minds?
I bolt, purblind, past a neatly arranged line
Gathered behind a snack counter, by books
Tampered with and abandoned, like toys
Ravished by curious children, to be reduced
Or given to the needy deaf and dumb.
Two flights pass me by as I walk down
The ascending escalator. I decline entertainments
And unbenign speculations that infect the brain.

When I am outside again, the air explodes my lungs with heat,
Exhaust, and caustic remarks from delivery boys
Unloading poultry cartons and unbinned fabrics
From transports mated blatantly to loading docks.
The day drops quickly onto the city, and now
I see a pendulum swinging where the Gulf should be.
The need to flee this city grows intolerable,
But the mind resists. Something about these people,
Who loiter headlong into dusk, attaches itself to me.
What do they possess, this feckless brood of gulls?

I retreat. The park is still filled with people
Caught in rapt inattention, though that band
Has long since retired. The man behind idiot grins
Leans, stationary, against the tree, laughing alone.
The sedentary one flips a page, concentrates,
Then hides inside his curling leaves and sighs.
Something. I know something is yet missing.

Will there be time? Will there be time to resign
From the cluttered mind to distanced objectivity?
Can I find behind a glass of blended whiskey,
When the shore fills up with listless gulls
And the submerged sun pumps water into tides,
The things that defy inspection? Must I decide
Tonight? Must I decide which items I bought today
With my imagination, when lambent city lights
Ride crescent islands beyond the cottage porch?

My stomach churns, and its hungry mind
Makes widening wakes as I leave this city.
Something refuses to let me loose. Invisible strings
Pull against my motion. Necessity eats my guts.
Another me struts before the windshield. I stop
Where no red light appears, apprehended by notions
That bear no relation to interpretations I crave.

Returning is a feckless exercise for me;
I have compromised something. Compassion lapses
Like Greek messengers run through for evil news
They oracularly convey from call to duty only.
The shore is a cemetery I pace absentmindedly.
*

Cold wash on my sandaled feet burns the toes,
And further retreat is impossible. I throw off my shirt,
Go slowly into the onshore breeze, which blows
With singular intent against my chest. I stretch,
Straining the biceps, wrenching the constrained torso,
Boasting contorted definitions of myself that screech
Painfully inside me like rusted windlasses.

I am youth. I am reckless spirit and intellect.
I am energy and full-bodied determination.
But what is it that in this fetid place
Splays the mind with unglazed greyness?
I go far up the diminishing corridor.
Gulls trace my carrion steps, expecting reward,
But my words spit upon the crowded air,
Curse them with boring self-commiseration;
I have lavished off others' beggaries too long.

A bristly wafer runs above my head; the goat
Slides in and out of the eyes like an illusive dime.
No suns of former days pursue themselves in shells
That rush up to slice my toes, and I stall,
Wanting to drink in the entire Gulf, to spit it out
Upon all that is dying or about to be dead.
I . . . I am very youth. I am such body
That nothing can contain me, and yet I am me.

I turn. The gulls have dispersed. The sodden sand
Has eaten shells. I near the cottage. I am . . .
I hear a rasping sound: tinfoil unrolled, ripped off,
And stretched gratingly over me. *Was* is me,
And I am trapped inside myself like a buried clam.
All along the fuzzy shore, horseshoe crabs,
Their fragile, crackly shells intact,
Pock the paths I follow. Jellyfish,
Flabby as cellophane bags filled with dirty clothes,
Wallow in menacing battlement. I see death.
Dead things are singling me out, unexplainably.

I wonder, now, what drew me out from the Gulf
To that pungent, venereal city today,
Only to bring me back to this stinking place.
*

Can it be I've squandered some provision?
No matter. There will be time to reconsider
The bitter decay I see in others and to learn
From mistakes and faulty calculations they've made.
This is no place to take detours or make of delay
A salable pastime. It's child's play to contemplate
Others' hasty retreats from themselves.
I am very youth. Who would barter his life
For grosser considerations? They were . . . I am I . . .

Yet, as I go inside, I wonder has some simplicity
Been compromised? Could I have left undone
Something of necessity? I see *was* and *will be*
Grappling for my thighs, wrestling me into *am not*.
I see myself inside the whiskey bottle, or image,
Floating upendedly, immersed in darker substances.
I tilt, pour myself out of glass into clearer glass.
My lips toast me, and I imbibe, and I am I and me,
Simultaneously. Something burns my insides.
I drown, swallowed alive in my own inebriation.

Clyde Griffiths' Chrysalis [‡]

Simulacra shimmer down shafts
Where elevators, like discarded cartons,
Await decay. Registered guests
Hide inside green decanters
Or under covers while maids make beds
Over them. Animals out of steaming showers
Slip tips for whiskey through door slits.
One-night couples take their dinners
Under glass. The hotel creaks,
Leaning away from the windy street,
Where debris passes for shiftless people.
This is one of the posh retreats
For litter-making creatures, a dream
Inside of life, self-contained, complete.
God, mother! If you could only see
The limousines and hear the easy change
Rearranging itself in my pressed pockets.
This is the life for me

[Morality gapes through the bars,]

Morality gapes through the bars,
Aping itself in other humans,
Who stare antically
All of a Sunday afternoon.
Too soon it will be too late
To imitate behaviour
That paces quadrupedally in cages
All of a spring zoo afternoon.
Temptation, a bisexual stripper,
Prates on condemned stages
Minors are forbidden to watch.
Participation in the mating thing
Comes in the youngest places
All of a sensual afternoon.
Is there no cure for modernity,
That vile creature, that lion
That wears its hair scruffy
And shares its harems polygamously?
Don't ethics, illusive fancies
Dreamed up by nonpracticing agnostics,
Count for anything other than love
All of a new generation?

Beginnings

My mind starts with beginnings,
A trickle from the spring
That tickles pebbles
In Itasca State Park.

I am Mississippi's head,
Hydroptique,
A river's cryptic brainwashing.
What I see
Issuing from a miracle
As I leap from puddle to muddled puddle
Is embryonic geography.
I imagine growth here,
Where I peer into opaque crystals
I bridge by stones.
Circles too perfect to contain death
Ripple to tourists' gazes,
And here is neither beginning
Nor any end to the natural phase
That hides in history books
And almanacs of other rainy days.

I am fabled Finn's river,
Upon whose widening banks
Hannibal paused to reflect,
Bloodhounds and townspeople
Failed to detect Nigger Jim
Hiding on the moving island
That knew no colored twain,
And Clark and Lewis
Began their inland trek,
Père Marquette settled forts
Along stray shores, where Indians
Chanted over burial mounds.

Bingham's flatboat men
Stopped here to watch their barks
Collect grey shadows under keels,
And side-wheelers slapped waters
Up and down, from Saint Louis to Cairo,
Memphis, Vicksburg, and New Orleans,

Queens in clapboard and belching stacks,
Pouring dust upon the land,
Navigating illusory undertows and sand bars,
Carrying elite to Basin Street
And even with the Natchez Trace;
The Gateway to the West wrested here,
Its monumental courthouse steps
Tongues decrying prejudice,
Vociferous obstacles to man's duress.

My mind grows like creation,
From pebble to Delta,
Beginning again in tomorrow's eyes,
Ending again where I began.

THE FOUL
RAG-AND-BONE SHOP
1969

For
Charlotte and Saul,

my
mother and father

This Pendent World

Trumpets blend; wars end inside the ears.

The searing heat dissolves;
Eyes empty as rifled safes swing on rusted hinges;
Limbs, like worms, squirm deeper into upturned earth,
And widows walk home to dress.
Those who once loved on private heaths
Weep, reach out to retreating crowds.

In defeat, Satan's crew hisses
                         exultantly.

The Foul Rag-and-Bone Shop

Such a night as never followed Pharaoh's curse,
Worse than the blight witch doctors watched,
Breathes over this Gulf apartment, its only child.
We hide inside, bastard pride of TV lions.
Fog, pervasive as persuasive Reichstag rhetoric,
Envelops sensibilities, blinds police and highwaymen,
Who pursue each other in ever-widening circles,
Until the hunted and the chaste leave off the chase,
Disgracing their occupations with compromise.

A snippet of lightning, like a newsreel clipping,
Slips through night's projector, struts comically
In ragged burlesque. No victims hiss the villain.
The tides ride in, their voices choralling hymns
Beneath the porch. We have nothing to reward
These unseasonable minstrels except blind submission.
Yet they persist in laying gifts at our feet,
Repeating the ritual, there in pantomime (welling pause),
Here in raucous chants against the shore's drugged skin.

Somewhere along the beach, an air-raid siren
Screeches a trinity, then hovers ubiquitously
At the ears' extremities, reminding me
Of London under a hungry blitzkrieg.
I arise. My eyes follow me, willing to leave
The fluorescent screen, whose images coalesce
In blessed falsifications. Down on the street,
Ponderous machines from another age stampede
Toward a conflagration's smoldering source,

And I can't return to the apartment's warmth,
Where the other three languish behind whiskey
And abbreviated soliloquies. Something calls me
To the weed- and kelp-strewn beach out back.
I follow to the wet edge, where coiling waves
Fester like leprosy over black-furry skin.
At once, I see purblind images roiling in light.
Silence overwhelms my raw speculations.
I await, wondering whether a newer day will whine,
Hesitate, then suckle off night's dark teats.

Indian Summer

These trees stand clumped in lumps of plum
And tawny beige; through this land I knew
In youth, soothing hues renew themselves.
Music of maple and walnut, sweet gum, elm
Overwhelms the eyes in cool reprise.

Yet with all this beauty, the leaves
Fluting earthward are sermons preached
On other altars in other seasons.
The funereal pomp of Donne's "Autumnall"
Rumbles the casket of an old man's mind.

An Anatomy of the Believer: The Twenty-Sixth Anniversary

Wherein, by occasion of the symbolic death of
Louis Daniel Brodsky, the frailty and
the decay of traditional faith
is represented

His shelves,
With countless colored faces,
Dilate like birds in flight.
Their varnished wings
Fling insults at his yawning.

These lettered spines,
Those mouths and lidded eyes
Withhold personality from him
As he tries to pry apart
This four-jawed vice.

Memory, like nervous drops of rain,
Splatters against storm windows.
He is witness to disintegration
That washes his murky brain.

Accumulation has made him slave
To wisdom that demands manumission
From this six-by-eight cave
He calls Plato's immolated grave.

Though he fingers his chin,
There are no more contemplative poses
In this world, where art and Scripture,
Like the self-deposed children of Moses,
Have chosen the harlot's namesake.

He finds no new themes to scribe,
And the tortured Saxon rhymes
That line his mind's back streets
Like scarecrow row houses at night
Cocoon his stillborn insecurities.

He feels precariously forsaken,
Having curbed his appetite
To include only older forms of learning.
He suspects no rewards
*

From fashioning oneself as a martyr
When poverty fattens the bones,
Chastity finds neither majority
Nor obedient few who raise a voice,
And forbearance gets no extension
On debts incurred in Monte Alverno.

The books' sacred words taunt him.
He, like Alcibiades, has vacillated
Too often between antagonistic factions.
The precepts conjoin to defeat him
Where he sits, a ravaged go-between,
At stalemate. Self-consciousness
Stones him. The ancients arbitrate,
Throw his clothes to hovering buzzards.

He goes naked among vacant lands,
Whose desolation mocks his vacancy.
But no Oedipus fleeing some curse
Waits, where four roads intersect,
To slay him, and his library,
This descendant of the house of Atreus,
Decries his defection, defies inspection
That might set his own house in order.

Nero, like an unwilling Virgil,
Escorts him to the right hand of Erebus.
But his insulation stays the flames,
And he awakens from prolonged yawning.

When confusion puts pressure on him
To draw conclusions or make excuses
For himself, he caresses with faith
Sacred revelations of unseen things.
From his cluttered shelves, he takes
A ruffled Bible, whose poppy-scented ways
His eyes have passed a hundred times.
Blessed confinement comforts him,
While the days lengthen his wrinkles
From one end of night into the next.

Morning's Companion

Once more,
for Jan

From this sandy bunk on an August morning,
Where hunks of color funnel down through dawn
To buff the corners of a day in the rough,
I feel the body's unrepeated shiftings
And its dry dreams drifting to lighter degrees,

Until something like the child's slow smile
Settles to a tabernacle inside the eyes.
Sweetest surprise outrides the minute hand,
Returns to the upright birth of breath,
And in a sculpted gesture of gentleness,
The future wife of a newer man
Bends down to caress the artist her kiss creates.

A Newer Consummation

For Jan,
in February

Windows rimpled with ice and frost
Reflect their ministrations
Against an opaque, outside night.
Like projections of infected cells,
They fester in their own undoing.
An unconscionable hiatus
Separates their youth from lateness.

Behind the earlier hours,
Before night severed itself
From their twin umbilici,
They'd sealed themselves in birth,
Howled voiceless elegies
In praise of unphrased verses
That curse them now with fatigue.

The bed creaks under slender weight.
The meek are spirited from sleep.
Viperine tongues lash out below,
Climb brass gunwales that coffin them.
No children of God ride its shoulders
But victims of spectral floods,
Whose blood is mottled with iceberg clots.

Was it sublimation
Anchored to floating islands
That grew maggots from unspawned kisses
Or a ululation of hungry lust
That ate its way to decayed surfaces?
Abject nakedness clothed them
In perversities Adam never knew.

She complains. His frantic restraint
Navigates falls where salmon writhe;
He swarms in crowded vacancies.
No mere physical notions, no sibilances
Scribbled down her upturned spine
Can unhinge the mind's conclusions.
They're caught in the net's wet twine.

Why did they come all this way
Only to write epitaphs in cemeteries
Where history's foolish Tenorios
Sprawl ignobly as captive slaves?
Was there ever an hour this evening,
He dourly wonders, when fecklessness
Wasn't baiting them unchecked?

Now, the hand that stayed him
Swims unexplainably through the sheets
And, like original clutching in space
That undid hiatus with less darkness,
Divides myriad newer firmaments.
His hand slides into her palm's halo,
Making silhouettes of an echoing silhouette.

Song

For Jan,
in White Cross

Mid-September drips into another winter
Faster than a ship listing slowly
Between fathoms of opaque aloneness.
Jan has returned to outlive this rain.

Elms come unattached from space
While leaves scrape yellow off the soggy air,
Then sift the colors of her floating eyes
And thread her lashes with silver-fine.

A sudden sun unlatches the castle gates,
Scatters her garden with art-glass roses.
Even the snow's chemistry, unconceived,
Is cameoed in the scald of her perpetual heat.

Indian cold grows narrow on the horizon.
Souls clothed with autumnal penumbra
Press close in blessed confessionals,
Awaken to a consecration of Jan's whispered kisses.

Zealous Voices

On the fatal shooting of a Negro teenager, alleg-
edly brandishing a pistol from his back pocket
while handcuffed and guarded, by two metro-
politan police officers.   St. Louis, Mo., 1966

Defectors, protectors,
And scandalized insurrectionists
Protest before Court 109.
The magistrate slams the door,
Declines their insults
And lewd replies. "You have no right!"
They shout. "Screw you," he says.
"There's no room in here for you
To obstruct scrupulous mainsprings
Of jurisprudence. The process
Must run its own due course,
Divorced from indignation
And publicly vulgar representation."

Outside, the group belches, curses,
Then disperses behind next morning's
Uncontroversial headlines to learn
That they, not the circumstantial men
Defended on thirdhand accounts,
Have been cited as the greatest threat
To a law-abiding citizenry.
Then each, without delay, puts away
His mutual redresses, digresses
Into horoscopic debates with himself,
Hoping to go incognito
Behind an aegis of individuality.

The Achieve Of

Dormitories are full of children
Too old for home and other conveniences
Though too untried for menial lives
That kick environmental walls
With foetal ineffectuality.
Class schedules and tuition checks
That bear little relation to work
Their endorsees have known firsthand
Get neatly filed by clerks
In the dean's and bursar's offices.
Dorm singles and suites are reclothed
With bric-a-brac and untimely slogans
Cut from *Realist* and *Mad* magazine
And tacked to walls scrawled in lipstick,
Where fictional Kilroys were last year.
Once order is replete,
They can make their ways
Through a thousand grey Decembers
And slide viperine among salacious leaves
That sift daily Aprils of sensuality.

How fine it is returning,
When routine tilts with inexperience.
For those who know the ropes,
The freedom of easy-patterned pressures
Pothers no one seriously.
This is the life in a once-time,
Brothers, sisters of the golden slime.
There's no need to reason why
Or to try your wings too assiduously.
To sport factional winds,
Where dissidence spawns behind beards
And sandals and gold-rimmed spectacles,
Is to bury yourselves under dissonant plots
Of self-consciousness. A weariness of things
Only rings true to dreary imaginations.
See each day as a pageant of hours,
As a thing of fecund immediacy.
Hear its quainter shades rippling ivy
And Indian rain trees,
Where breezes part space for persistent suns.

Accept that freedom before these years
Exchange you for tedious transactions.
Be able to say you've won something
Autumnal days can never take away
Nor dissipate. For whoever's heard rain
Inch down drainpipes to a full bin
Beneath the eaves and listened
To a groaning freight train
Hollow out tunnels of slower nights
Or seen a tanker's rusty hull
Bulging with too much grain
Must know the meaning of completion.

Cycles

Somewhere back of the sky, within a floating seed,
A child stands at the edge of warmest birth,
Emerges to plant the winds with crying words.
A whitely woman, waiting at the end of night,
Untangles vines that climb ripening runners,
Until man, blessed instrument of love, arrives.

A crisp, clear stillness chills the wet leaves,
Fills the ears with insistent whispering of years
Distant from this path, lawn, house of careers
Called life. And this poignancy is air, idea,
Philosophy born of purest carvings in a tree
Screened against the shimmerings of unseen wind.

Phantasms of Sleep

From The Garden of Cyrus,
Sir Thomas Browne

Leaves of the silver-maple tree
Turn down, anticipating rain
That crouches in the sated west.

Beyond the lop-eared crests
That whine on certain nights
With echo-broken sounds
Of vagrant, outbound trains,
An unwound sun runs down.

A lady masked in topaz lace
Paces across a waning sky,
Reclines in a naked chasm.

Rain rumbles from tumid wombs,
Tumbles through fetid eventide
To line the spider's cable-stitch,
And now the leaves fall down
Upon the rabbit's matted back.

A girl undresses behind my eyes,
Touches me from a sifting leaf,
Sprays me with a seething rain.

Ishmael

Buoyed up by that coffin, for almost one whole day and night,
I floated on a soft and dirge-like main. . . . On the second day,
a sail drew near, nearer, and picked me up at last. It was the
devious-cruising Rachel, that in her retracing search after her
missing children, only found another orphan.
— Herman Melville, *Moby Dick*

I

I searched Cíbola's seven cities
For gold, charted Phoenician states
In hope of discovering Cathay
And richer trade routes further east.
I tasted of de León's glades
Without encountering his fountain
And anchored off western Hesperides,
Though no Tithonus broke from sleep.
Twice I passed Tenerife and the Cape,
Went beyond the Pillars to Atlantis
And back, once settling near Pompeii,
Until black wax molted pagan bones.
I crossed temporal divides,
Trying to reside near fairer temples
In cities swaddled in warmer climes,
But monuments erected themselves,
And all was not well anywhere.
Now, I alone am left, though the tale
To be told necessarily escapes me.

II

Aye, and there's the timeless rub.
Inhibitive forces ply me. Royal Societies
Require my assistance as living proof
To skeptics that one such as me
Has survived their untried projections.
Academies soothe me with pedagogy,
While I, dizzy from maddening heights,
Dangle from science's vocal folds,
A Jonah in a thousand larynxes,
Unable to approximate my own sound.
Printers, clinics, juggling troupes
Seek my freakish company.
*

Misery would marry me at once. Aye,
But there's no time for compromise
When all's not well in Terra Firma,
Where temples erect themselves in effigy.
My discoveries go cold as seas
In deepest winter.
I should have been that wretched whale.

III

Of late, I've paused with quainter shades
In Padua, Oxford, and Alcalá.
In Rome, in Avignon, I sat with God,
Wore periwig and costume frock
In courts with reason at their side.
Now I'm the world's specious cash.
Counterfeit crosshatchings undermine me;
My spurious currency is spent.
Balance comes unfavorably,
Though what I demand is abundantly cheap.
Are there no profiteers out for booty?
I could be pickled brine or salted pork,
Sold by the hogshead. I might be water,
Precious water, saved in staved barrels.
Yet who would squander their last doubloon
When prosperity crowds the sensibility,
Hearts and brains bleed in meat markets?
That I were son of the *Rachel*'s captain,
Suspended in humors of cold affection!

The Nuptial Bower

For my sister Babs

Over this whole frozen lake down here,
Where no motorboats skim,
Propellers still snag a former breeze;
Cotter pins sift through oblique waters
Like leaves coming undone in winter air.

A man and wife come down to the snow line
At the edge of no lake
To share each other's implausible lips.
Inside the fish shack,
By a dry fire,
No one spies that sidelong embrace,
Which belongs to the man with implausible wife.

The lake spawns no fish, no ice.
No water fills these banks; they overflow.
The fish shack burns; it never was.
Somewhere, the man and his naked wife
Gather up leaves that have decomposed
And lie down beneath no trees to sleep.

The Turning In

For Ladd,
who has taught me to see,
on his sixty-sixth birthday

The sky is an architect's cardboard display,
Layer piled up and splayed upon layer
As though someone would have it redesigned.
A small plane walks across the horizon,
Its drone prevailing over the locusts' moan,
Which follows me like a lonesome ghost.

I am noises;
I am voices that crowd this thick night air,
Sounds that crack the malforged ears.

I am, in July,
The quail's unsung "bob-white" or peach trees
That squeak deeper each season into the earth,
Grass matted under feet, roaches in dank repose.

What I see is me,
For I am every rotting object I perceive
Through the mind's dried-out melon leaf,
Or each fleshly thing that grows and dies
In this tangled patch, where the coon lies fat.

What I am is tumid root
Without its fruit, vine void of writhing food,
Severed stalk leaking milk-white juices,
Pink-diminishing odors of the mimosa's bloom,
Shadows swept out by the pine's full broom,
The ribald scent of steaming horse and hog.

In this antique store behind my heart,
Nature's dusty faces clog shelves with dross;
They peer out at me through untouched cracks,
Through unfilled fissures in need of repair;
They stare as though I might come back
To rejuvenate these legacies of summers past.

Taps

Day is done.
The roads are muddy
And loose as no-colored putty.
Who can see, when mist
Whispers through pines and spruce,
Where the breeze should be,
Beyond the windshield's scope?
Who unleashed this wetness?
What wild wizard would belch
This slobber-drunk night,
Mindful of no-people out for love
Or discovery?
We pass through that glass
Like undefined memories in gauze,
Outclassed by nature
And a god no eye could find.

Gone the sun,
Behind birch and virgin pines,
Dispersed like dead air
Before a pair of fans
Whose chopping blades are razors.
We drive where the light was,
Swerving for dead raccoons
And fabulous jumping frogs
That escape haunt-clogged swamps
No humans infest.
Is this that source where pests
Demand painful conversation
And radical explanation to simplicities
Adam was warned against by Raphael?

From the lakes
To ten thousand other forsaken bodies,
We gambol, swilling blended whiskey
And boilermakers in flight.
This ragged, mist-spitting night
Challenges us like the wicked witch
In search of oven fodder.
Why was Hitler a male witch?
Do Jews make good gingerbread men?
Cookies spoil in dank cellars;
Their faces break, brittle as bones,
In crispy furnaces of the imagination.

From the hills
We come, to further hills that spill
Like daredevil barrels
Over the lip of this lake.
Can't you hear the waves there,
Paring themselves against the shore
Like demons' nails on circular saws?
There's a war growing tumescent
Beyond that last hill, toward which
We go, now, slow as lemmings
That doubt their own motivations.
There it is, that ear-breaking lake,
Superior to none but itself this night.
Where are the million blighted souls
Who fight in swamps and rice fields?
(I saw a real Indian yesterday,
Dressed anachronistically in war bonnet,
Offering handfuls of unshred wild rice
To customers come to gorge themselves
On All You Can Eat For Three Dollars.
"God, Mom! It's a real Indian!"
Bastards that laughed and touched him!
Buffalos and whooping cranes are less
Extinct.)
Who will send the slant-eyed freaks
Weeping in agony for deeds done
In some combustible notion of freedom?
Don't they know that freedom is word,
That words are rationale for lack of action?
Action is neither walking with a gun
Nor stunning crowds with rhetoric.
I am an anti-semantic gingerbread man.
I act in the name of others,
Those brothers of the slime and mire
Who load their minds' quags
With boisterous folly.
Who can let them go unnoticed,
When night spreads over itself,
Like orgiastic reptiles just hatched,
Four horsemen who ride with scythes?

From the sky
Lightning fails to break the mist.
There's something frightening when air
Shares the nostrils' passageways
Like too many people crowding
Fallout shelters on a calm day.
Something hangs distrustful out here,
Where water and vapor coalesce
As though night's shroud might never lift,
Darkness never ascend to daybreak,
Nor midnight ever come again.
We gather driftwood from the beach,
Tossing up decay on littered decay.
What were once trees now explode,
Join the fire's ravagement,
And here is light burning off,
Drilling temporary holes
In this raucous, antic-filled screen.
Who has seen a shell blast a bluff?
Who can hope to stay catastrophe?
People! People! Can't you see it?
Discreet politicians who drink milk
Can't tell you the simple nontruths.
A curse descends on them,
And the end cries for recognition.
Who can tell this colossal wreck
That what the world needs now
Is to slow down and take stock?
The earth's shelves are cluttered;
Things and things spill off them,
And inventory comes later each year.
Somebody has been pinching things.
(I saw a house so filled with china
No bull could have got through the door.)
And where is the bull turned buffalo?
There's a distinction to be made here
Between extinction and survival;
I refer you to the word "revival"
In the Thorndike daily stock return.

All is well
Somewhere, where neutrality flourishes,
Jack and Jill still trudge to apexes,
And the King of France
No longer dances with himself.
(Hear tell, he wears nothing underneath
Except a terminal case of leprosy.)
But now he shakes, casts dice, rolling
In the name of Lot's sacred lot.
Sodom erodes like Mexican soil,
And hotels sink eight feet each year.
Can't you hear the crumbling dirt
Suffocating worms and steel piles?
When will the Queen of the Adriatic
Dissolve into static grots of cold mud?
And where is the King of France now?
Why, he and the cow are after Bo-peep,
But the haystacks are creeping away
Like Indians on plains with trees
For feathers stuck in their skulls.
The salt lick burns; eyes leak blue ink.
Who can think about new lands,
When these sands we stand on now
Refuse our drunken, reeling weight?

"Safely rest,"
They say at revival meetings,
When repentance comes hard as hell
And hell breaks like laboring dusks
Over forests on fire.
We try to look out over this misty water.
That city is there somewhere,
A hidden anchorite covered with scabs.
Cabbies in the city have quit their hacks.
The people fear another crash.
Didn't stocks fall once and people leap,
Landing on two-legged lemmings
On their way to defunct banks or
Atop cranks about to assassinate presidents?
Glad I brought this blanket to sleep on.
*

Who ever heard of a twenty-five-year-old
From a filth-spoiled family in Shaker Heights,
Grosse Pointe, drawing a pallet on nothing
But sand and empty beer cans
Crushed by the inebriated hand of disorder?
(Just the other night, I talked with Dante.
He said he'd taken out all his cash
And stashed it behind the eyes, in vaults
Where no one with parasites
Could undermine his bad conscience.
He'd write his own obsequies, he told me,
When there was more than a beggar's chance
To dissent.) What is change but suffering
Yourself to outlive calumniation?
Was there ever a rebel born of contentment?

God is nigh,
But the people in high places
Disgrace themselves
Believing they know what's going on.
Here where I sit, trying to find sleep,
The world rages about my naked chest,
The throat cracks like quarry mud,
And elements whisk about my dreams
Like tubercular angels from Walpurgis lands.
The dimming fire lights portions of me,
While a god looks on with bewilderment.
The fire flickers; flames are swallowed alive.
To repent is impossible here on this plot,
Phony as the Lone Ranger's rendezvous clump.
Sand and air, fire and water simmer,
And my eyes, like unpredictable geysers,
Cry, though no people buy tickets
To witness nature's wonders.
Where is that land, and the end of days,
Where all is calm and filled with grace?
Are there pastures beyond here
Where sheep jump walls and scurry away
Without worry of monkeys hanging from trees?
Who can hope to try God's patience,
*

When we refuse the sages' insight?
God alone can refuse us — fools
Who prejudice each other for tradition's sake.
But somewhere, that slinking creature
Crouches, awaiting his chance to start fires
Boiling once more the hot blood of dinosaurs.
We lie in the balance.
Alchemists play with our values,
And nothing has any worth.
Whores run rampant through streets.
Black faces rob stores for payment,
Though remuneration falls short by centuries.
Bordellos exact dignity from our billfolds,
But there are no more gold backs. Silver dollars
Are scarce, and Kennedy halves are toys
For speculators' soaring greediness.
Why can't a pound of feathers
Weigh more than Galileo's golden pebble?
I know. He knows, too. It's you and me
And all the ships at sea that founder
When the scales are tipped and trumps
Finesse themselves in suspect crossruffs.
There He is, in the waves out there!
I can see Him in the eye of the lake,
Hear Him in night's bristly ears
Listening to me listening to Him
Move in, taking His cautious time.
The fire spins high, bellows, then crawls
Inside charred logs wet as dawn and dies.
The sand under my stomach goes flat,
And somehow, I can live with myself out here.
Can it be that death and its antipode
Thrive side by side in certain minds
That entertain notions of immortality?
Can I ever return to my quarters in town?
Will they know I'm different or see me
Still as of that same tired species
That dies, each night, inside itself?

The Burning Off

I

A near V of foraging sea gulls
Deviates from tedious formation,
Strafing shore-bound ebbs.
Sandpipers scurry faster than field mice,
Nipping at stray diatoms and plankton;
They hurry to elude waves that slobber
Impatiently as apple-foaming horses
Against the glutted beach, then turn
To join a million fallings away.
Along the bleached stretch of land
That bars hotels and walled resorts
From water, flaccid jellyfish
Wallow in their own diameters;
Barnacled shells hear themselves
Grinding away in millennial lassitude;
Horseshoe crabs pock the pumiced sand,
Their brittle skeletons, their tails
Tilting like useless dragon quills,
Menacing even in rigid demise.
And as I go, hands behind my slowing motion,
Eyes tracing prints of fowl and human trek,
Something, the voiceless breeze perhaps,
Reminds me night is coming again.

II

Not so far out that the mind,
If it so inclined, couldn't lift a hand
And touch, the circular furnace
Bends down to sear a burning horizon.
I turn so near in to its core
The eyes exclude all former notions
Except residue of the listing day.
(I see two men inside that mass,
One working a bilge feverishly,
The other stoking boilers with acetylene.)
Who made that hole that ingests you,
Sun? Will you extinguish yourself
Or, like a Halloween apple
*

String-dunked in a molasses vat,
Reappear with a more enticing coat
When dawn draws you up into day?
The eyes blink once, and when I search,
All has disappeared but a single smear:
Cinnamon spread in ripples over toast.
Far off, down both outrushing corridors,
Flecks that could be other people
Seep into the brilliant dusk. I am left,
A ghost among ghosts going cold,
Bereft out here in a cemetery.
I have buried something of myself.

Introit

Autumn leaves fall like deer hooves
Off the breeze's speedy feet.
Summer closes its eyes and sleeps
Under a lumbering muscatel sky.
The dry creek that bracelets this land
Is a precious antique; no griefs
Lie beneath its serene patina.

A dry-wood fire is quietly consumed
Inside an outdoor pit. Pious flames,
A cardinal's embroidered surplices,
Twist high into the atmosphere,
While its smoke, the unkempt beard
Of a parishioner come to Eucharist,
Veers low as if to kiss his feet.

In this valley no city has fortified
Nor man been forced to compromise,
Nature has set aside her prize.
This is a garden of graceful repose,
Where creatures pace and people go
To expose the ghost they closely hide:
That love which He alone can know.

FDR Drive and 78th Street

Landlocked atop the cement abutment,
He is free to breathe the river's salt,
To see the gulls mediate both bridges.
His feet hang listlessly above the water.
Beneath his stolid vigil, he watches bottles,
Half-submerged, bobbing toward the Battery,
Rancid cans tottering like drunks they fed,
And matches he hurls catch the breeze
Before consummating their downstream course.
A Tracy tug looms faintly north of time,
Then takes the bend, nudging its barges
Beyond him in coupled recession.
Again, the river slows behind its banks;
Its tireless flow subdues trucks and cabs,
Fast-spanning cars, cycles, and vans
That chase each other along the Drive.

Beyond his perimeter, a jet sails low,
Falling through slack air of a landing path.
Overhead, a copter chops the wind apart,
Rattles his rib cage, then disappears,
While the sky and water wait for silence.
In this thick congestion that is night,
He sees activity at the white hotel:
The swinging doors, cars that loiter in line,
The working girls and prostitutes
And misguided Carries, who emerge
To be swallowed alive by this saw-toothed city.

His sedentary omniscience overwhelms him.
He is Homer's fisherman at eight bells,
Racing toward the lee of a Gloucester shore,
Or Thoreau waiting for the Fitchburg train
To break his amber quietude.
Nothing eludes him except the pious bum
Who comes out of nowhere to beg a dime.
When he turns into those porcelain eyes,
His own reflection detects him.
Once, he would have waited here
For a dark, decent girl to appear.

The Well

I climb up the well
That's bored within my drowsy head.
Its moss-cobbled walls
Barely support my heels and toes.
I have passed this night down here
Up to my knees in silt and fungus,
Among splintered rabbits and fowl.
No water has filled this cylinder for years.

During the night, accidental trespassers,
Guarded from specters and reckless insects
Within their lanterns' penumbras,
Must have placed these planks
That lid the opening, where light just drips.
I can't budge the intractable cover
Above my head. Precarious balance
Teases me. My arms span the diameter.

But I am no Samson, and these dank walls,
Pillars that buttress the worm-burrowed earth
Of my unfurrowed fields, don't yield.
Am I Leonardo's frozen humanist,
Head hung in painful repose, naked legs
Groping between middle-aged darkness?
Only the hands' diminishing strength
Keeps me from another descent.

The Personal Creation

On discussing the merits of Calvert
blended whiskey with Essie,
1/28/67

I

The mind fills up with psychedelic smoke,
Goes blind as time in spherical cyclotrons,
Trying to open up the last three thousand years.
What would older minds have thought
Confronting an unperceptive Socrates on dope?
How can the brain resurrect residue
Tired imaginations can't fire up
Yet refuse to set loose in garbage cans
Where you and I beg for food and weekly news?

II

That's the way it is here,
Where any little high-school teacher of twenty
Can tell pupils she'd spit in the President's face,
When Jewish bartenders outwit the FBI.
The national disgrace is anywhere where people
In high places serve up idioms on silver trays
And ransacked clichés on china-lined Melmac.
It's all in the *Doomsday Illuminations.*

How does a person know to call it quits,
When milkmen and Sunday-school teachers
Of Judeo-Christian persuasion
Inculcate younger minds with prejudice
And unscrupulous political rubrics
They know so little about? It's not right
To hide away in cork-lined shacks on Laputa,
No matter how unprostituted the word you preach.

III

The rope that holds the foundered ship in tow
Shreds, slips its capstan; the bow sinks deeper,
Until there's no hope to save the boat from worms
And urchins that swarm below pacific seas.
Are there no engaging purposes for us to share
With unaging history's madrigal? Hey, you, Thucydides!
Aren't there any lessons to be taught
Or bought in paperback translation with pocket change?

I gloss reports that appear in weekly magazines,
Cases contested and brought before diapered courts
For libel that harms no familial dignities
Or calumnies that bear little resemblance to reality.
Extracurricular activities feed life with energy;
They alone single out metaordinary deeds we idolize.
It's honor, pride, derisive bitterness and courage,
Abstracted and dissociated from sensibility and light,
That form stalactites in the mind's chilled cave.

IV

The Gulf busts loose tonight. Unnatural light
Consorts with cripples and wheelchaired mermaids
Who wear scales where their groin should be.
Who can see into the spume and froth
When lightning cancels perception, signals doom,
And destruction hovers like a hungry buzzard
Looking for purchase on the brain's carrion?
These humans, a strange kind that worships itself:
Bastard dogs all, hypnotized by plate glass!

V

Which way does one turn when the ears burn
With wind's scurrilous trumpets and the eyes
Line uterine tubes of accidental space,
Collide with sperm traveling in threes and nines
That abort the inner perception and kicking truth?
It's the items and conventional ideas they feed us
That disturb humors, curb the intellectual appetite.
A strange kind that barters each other: sick lemmings
All, who sink back circumstantially into earth to be born!

Can you hear that horn scraping the ears' womb?
What unusual call to transmutation! Do you see
Those embryonic lemmings of unnatural cause
Growing tumescent within the human pupa? Soon,
They'll crawl walls where women in labor lie,
Then cry to be suckled, weaned on liquid fodder
Too hot for the latent butterfly. Only one
Each three hundred years becomes a flaming peacock.

But they thrive off the tree, beyond the gate,
In shadows on the western side, deprived of nothing
Save the Struldbruggs' wrinkled life. They writhe,
Slither among each other like new-hatched snakes,
Despising the form they take, the life that slows
In subtropical alphabets to an idiot's pace.
They're a classless race of faceless creatures,
Who eat each other with words not rooted in fact.

VI

Can you see that man with slatted ribs?
From him came helpmates too numerous to bear,
Whose fleshly names and hair belie their curse.
With their fish eyes turned inside out,
They see only themselves and pia-decay
That oozes in blood banks of confused speculation.
Peculation begat itself a tougher hide:
Self-consciousness under a shell of unnerved pride.
Narcissus died urinating his brains in a basin.

VII

Now the storm vies with weakness inside me.
I hear voices clamoring like lions in heat
From the crumbling peak of Ararat. Rack the balls
And break now, or forever hold your cue in hand.
Who cares what tutors taught you to play the game?
The fact remains that beggars never cheat
Except when pressed, nor wise men break from rest
Unless to watch stars falling in the west.
As for me, I have no serious doubts about anything
Except doubt itself and the sun arising in the east.

Land of the Setting Sun

A jealous sun beats hard the reef
And warps motels that line the beach,
While the aged sleep or pass their days
Playing heated games of shuffleboard.

From east and north these people come,
Effigies and maskers of darker suns,
Who hope to make some compromise
With failing sight and slow decay.

A man, or silhouette, in fatted tan
Stands with pole on the end of a pier,
Scanning mullet, catfish, and bass
That pass his bait for richer catch.

Perched on the sea wall not far away,
His wife crochets, adjusts her bonnet,
And, warned against the sun's disease,
Creams red legs to avoid poisoning.

An elderly lady gets wheeled about
By a spinster nurse in patient white;
She nods her palsy to silent guests,
Who breathe identical etiquette.

Though sandpipers play upon these shores
And kingfish and cobias flute greyer shades
That nuzzle beneath the water's wedge,
No humans pace the pockmarked sands.

I alone lie against hot sands,
Waiting on rays to burnish my skin,
Or walk the beach with tireless feet
From one end of day into the next.

I bathe in dreams, with de León,
Of pilgrims who came to stake a claim
Where history had taken preeminence.
My youth is wasted on fantasy.

I awaken just now to excited shouts
Of two blond children about my head,
Digging for shells, filling their pails
To buttress a fort by the swelling shore,

Whose waves no longer speak to me
(They have sluffed into feeble chorusings,
While the screeching gulls' soliloquies
Go out in muted cacophony).

Those shells are dying on the shore;
The ocean's roar in their coiling ears
Rolls back to sea like silent notes
Tuned in a vacuous continuum.

The pain of heat goes down from day,
And all retire into evening dress
Except for me. I feel the absence
Of absented things closing in on me.

47th Street West

Men carrying black suitcases,
Wearing de facto patrician noses
For frontlets between their brows,
Expose themselves to the crowds.
Traffic flows jagged as lightning;
Currents go against currents,
While these suspect shades
Masquerade wares from a hundred ports
For others with taximetered eyes.
Inside these Geneva retreats,
Compromise and agreement goad people
From Scarsdale, Grosse Pointe, Park Street,
Who pause tentatively at the door
For a right to partake of bargains
Only the rich can afford.

Their windows, identical in all but gender,
Are peacocks preening conceitedly
Or transvestites ending their stage routine.
Amethyst, jade, and stony topaz,
Like veins marbling bony fingers,
Line their yellowing display trays.
Cameos lifted from abandoned vaults,
Necklace halters of beaded crystal,
Like tubercles racing through blood,
Flood clutter-greedy imaginations.
Estate diamonds, rings, cultured pearls,
Stopwatches encased in platinum
Suggest conceptions of Rothstein,
Who wore stickpins and clips
Between ruffled shirt and wide, loud tie.

A bookstore, solitary as a Bedouin tent,
Reeks breath that never reaches the street.
Its window, a defunct Cyclopean eye,
Is bedizened with complete back issues
Of extinct magazines and posters
For poetry readings two years old.
Within, volumes molder in orange crates,
Toothpaste cartons, and on rented shelves
That shoulder history's promised failures,
*

Slapdash mysteries, classics, and myths.
Tourists stare. Peddlers share its awning.
An occasional collector finds its door.
In a graveyard lined with unknown lives,
This store is a monument among cenotaphs,
Whose genealogy increases with time.

Awakening

For Larry Millman

This is no great awakening,
No enlightenment, this morning,
When severed branches beyond the glass
Scratch the eyes' contours.

Someone must have declined grace,
Reasoned differently. Dawn has come
Without intervention, and light
Pierces shades no supplicants pace.

A cough rattles my clumsy frame.
Convenient tissues take the waste
My nose obstinately relinquishes.
The eyes forage themselves, naked.

Unregeneration wears this bed's sheets:
Togas that clothe inquiring Oedipus.
Light leaks facsimiles of its original,
Shares space with my body heat.

I sneeze. Winter engenders itself in me.
Freezing fingers, webbed duck feet,
Reach to touch their fleshly machine;
Covenant of skin and soul comes hard.

The traduced spirit hovers above itself.
I look on, dissociated from anticipation,
Taking no cues from morning's newness.
My palms rake the spine's perforations.

The back comes cautiously erect,
Hoisting ten hours off reclining night.
A bristly blight, prospect, descends,
And the end rushes up. Dreams crawl out

Like worms to inundated surfaces,
Seeking paradoxical refuge in thicker air.
Residual configurations confuse vision;
The eyes grapple with indecisions

That cry in this auctioneer's estate,
Whose posthumous codicil demands execution.
Thy will be done,
And I offer up myself to the highest.

My strewn trousers, nicotined shirt
Attest that someone lived here once.
My isolate spectacles, instruments of war,
Reflect blindness from their insular perch.

I see myself in their vitreous walls,
Hung to that oak behind the blinds.
My mind crawls down before its body,
But the tree grows continually skyward,

And I teeter in impartial weakness,
Too feeble to divide leafless partitions.
An incongruous cardinal lights on my limb,
Finds no feed on the eyes' window sills.

Yet light has filled this torpid room.
I must make my move, breathe life
Into abandoned relics of other moods.
A vagrant yawn impregnates the process,
And I, an exile, break from the gloom.

The Devil's Circus, Chicago, '68

For Jan,
in Miami

Spurious currency circulates,
Politicians worry,
And regular delegates lose their seats.
Outside, police widen the night,
Draw tight the vise about peaceful bodies;
Like foxes in traps,
Children bite each other,
Trying to free a limb to free themselves.

But the night belches.
    Locomotives churn out of roundhouses,
    Melting down the tracks,
    Burning away the sleepers.
People are fed in, all of them;
Then they are steam, air — they *were*,
And the machines run on, run out,
                imperviously.

Good Friday, 1965. Riding Westward

I

Several ideas at the same time
Held in suspension;
The poet's spine,
Sprung in rhythmic declension;
A static mind,
Burning off febrile tensions
That line vaults
Buried under convention;
Resuscitated designs
Make untraditional intervention.

II

Ears, like probing words,
Hug the ground,
Listening for the pounding monster
That spans Promontory's plains,
Not knowing that they, Indians
Of an older battle order,
Must submit to iron horses
No arrows can pierce for meat.
Their eyes, despising ideas of progress
They neither understand nor want,
Band together in renegade tribes,
Lost as deeds to lands
Forfeited for beads and spirit water.
See them now, folks, riding fire engines,
Sitting atop flagpoles, oil rigs,
Volcanic city halls, those few who knew black gold
Was worth more than presidential oaths
Endorsed by Teapot, slick-domed ministers
Whose constituencies refused to speak.

Those same eyes today, who can say
Where they might be if not for "machines"
And democracies by which white fathers
Swamped the senses
Under crepe patriotism and red tape,
Which flowed profusely as buffalo juice?
*

And what of their sacred totems,
Which no modern magicians can reconstruct
Or duplicate with mechanical templates?

Who knows what gods expired from lands
That dust bowls ravaged and perished miners
Trod in creaky Conestogas and Willys Jeeps,
Those same gods, phoenixes consumed in pyres
That know no end, that ride like pennons
Atop stacks of crude refining and cracking plants?
God! Who would exchange Manhattan today
For a nickel subway token, when Texas, Oklahoma
Are unspoken masters of a race of Houyhnhnms?

III

And over there, on thin invisible rails,
Windwagon Smith drifts behind his mizzenmast
Like some scurrilous Ahab driven by rage
Into the eye of some private cosmical debate.
He waves his hands, flying by, dropping seeds
Behind his disappearing geography.

He's seen defunct Indians on reservations
In Dry Gulch and Dead Man's Junction,
Had a shave and haircut for two bits
Behind cigar-store obelisks of ignoble savages
Made heroic years later by TV ratings.
Once again he takes to his wagon,
Trying to elude magnates with enough money
To endow museums with his accouterments.
His wagon skirts towns without insides,
Behind which hide court jesters and fools,
Scruffy stunt men and flunkies
With sawed-off Buntlines and 74s.

He reaches crests of Tahoe and Estes Park,
Plummeting from literary bluffs into climes
Restricted for mobile homes and Baker tents
With rents based on average national incomes.
But the windwagon needs refueling.
He'll have to make his grubstake and "get"
Or retire as local police chief or guide.

IV

Painless Peter Potter extracts teeth
For half-price, while his wife sews bows
And imitation-leather buttons on coats
Made "specially" for the local politico,
Seneca Doane, and other Zenith gentry.
Soon, the Potters will sell out
To open a shopping center in Gopher Prairie
For their growing clientele. Who can tell
What the future will hold, when Greeley,
A new-world Nazi, is selling for free
Ideas on peripatetics? "Little Chickadees,"
Clementine, Steinbeck, Claude Dukenfield,
And refurbished *Cimarron*s go very west.

Where are the legendary ones who made a name
For folklore and fame from deeds conceived
And recorded by teenagers and adolescent adults:
The Bowies and Boones, Crockets, Dillons and Jameses,
Who fled when elbowroom gave way to Hollywood?
"It can't happen here," said a certain Mr. Smith,
Forgetting to be prepared for corruption
And interruptions from his boy-scout duties.
"What guts!" some said, when he trained to D.C.,
Then drowned in Willet Creek — a senatorial Dante
Who couldn't forget what he'd seen
In the nation's Lethe. Lies! Unbelievable!

But that's what this country's founded upon:
Bedrock and ten-gallon bola ties and hats.
Don't knock it, buddy, if you ain't tried it!
It's the West, baby, safeguarded against poverty.
Prosperity reeks like dying cattle
Slaughtered right here before your eyes,
Behind rodeo pens and picnic grounds.
It's the open road, running untrammeled
Through Currier & Ives lithography
To the great ocean/sea Balboa claimed
And Frost transcribed. Take Brooklyn Bridge
And Eads! Let me have that Golden Gate
That opened to Jolson as Troy to Agamemnon's noise.

V

The poet flies westward on a whim,
His wings flapping out hollow words
On cool breezes of demise. This is our country.
Sing praise! Echo those golden strains!
It's the open-ended plains Frederick Church
And Remington stretched out on canvas;
It's a land unheralded ever before in the history
Of man. Don't you understand? It's freeways
And psychedelics and misguided Riding Hoods
And Heidis sleeping with rummies from the Hill.
Goddamn! Ain't that the berries?

Where else does one go to discover stardom, boredom,
Fish brought in on trawlers to your doorstep,
Campuses crowded with so much imagination
And drug-injected incantation and protestation?
It's here that the newer religions of Li Po
And Maharishi spawn on suburban lawns
And in beer grots and impoverished espresso bars.

We got it all right here, baby,
Right under your fingernail. All sails
To the winds! It's the promised land
Moses never knew firsthand. Understand
When I say this is the place, baby.
You can't beat it with a milelong hot dog.
We got that, too, if you ain't fatted calves.
Eat, drink, and feel Mary, for tomorrow ye diet!
It's the challenge. The sun grows bigger each year
On the garbage we leave to be carted away.

VI

Hey, hey! What say! *Carpe diem*, take it away!
Good God! Can you hear those cheering fans?
Can you see them standing up? Touchdown,
And a silvery fuselage shudders on rubbery gear,
Then whines into crowded silence, and you're here.
It's under three hours from ghost to ghost.
Unprecedented, baby; that's all I got to say.
*

Hotels, extravaganza, motels, and boatels;
Bonanzas on every corner owned by Zeckendorf,
Where delicatessens in Chinese neighborhoods
Do bang-up carry-out service to Steins turned Deans
And Leland Stanfords, né Olefskys, turned Simons again,
Each of them gospelers of wealth, anachronistic
Silas Laphams who refuse to give in to honesty,
Which might break them overnight. It's business, folks.
And there ain't no stoppin' it, I say.
Pray in your churches, just like always;
That's what they're there for. But don't forget
That to help the handicapped ain't good business.
That's just grass roots, baby, common knowledge.

Who's got the fastest gals in the West?
Dallas, SMU, or Southern Cal?
Stay tuned in to the halftime show
And postgame interview to learn the real truth.
But now let's take time out for station break.

VII

Just now, the sun is settling in the west,
And there seems a definite need for rest
From fatiguing endeavours that spend the mind
As profligates their precious inheritance.
It's a mild, sherbet-smooth night for sleeping,
And I'll drop all thoughts and sink secure
Into an unwrinkled bed with the wife and kid.
There's no sense fooling myself. That red ball
Out there — we're friends. In the cool morning,
I'll just step out on my patio above the bay,
Stand in my P.J.'s with a glass of O.J.,
A vitamin, Zentron, coffee and toast,
And shake hands with the host of another day.
Goddamn! What a great life they've made for us!

Visitation

A blessing for Jan

This day runs out
Like water from a slow drain,
And I awaken to view a new moon
Spray the Greater Ladle with a hazy glow.

Snow, like locks of baby hair,
Hides in pockets up there in that clear black eye.
Below night's timberline, I bend,
Ascending through naked ionospheres.

A hand or the shadow of a heated breeze
Sways me from sleep, unfreezes the seeds
That tree alleyways of forgotten dreams.
I climb inside a perfect whiteness.

Yet who ever hears the sacred flakes break
Without earthly choirs searing the ears?
Too, who has ever churched brittle fingers
And not feared the nearness of another's death?

The prolonged yawn bears subtle witness.

Rejection: The Legacy

For Moses truly said unto the fathers, A Prophet shall the Lord
your God raise up unto you of your brethren, like unto me.
— Deuteronomy 18:15

He took five steps
No wider than rib clefts
To cross the Stygian waters.
On that other side,
Where fat river horses
And leopard frogs
Slithered into rushes,
He lay facedown,
Weeping.

He was Moses, rejected.
The shattered tablets
He'd clung to for life
Were smeared with blood;
They'd cut his body
Like shears severing wire.
Behind him, across the flood,
Fugitive voices pierced his ears
Jeeringly:

"Sinner! Your promised land
Is where you lie. High treason,
Committed in the name of mercy
And right reason,
Shall be your crime.
You shall drink the sand
That swaddles you
Until your throat flakes dry
As dead fishes' scales."

He looked around, writhing,
In time to see the crowds
Dissolve into suburban houses,
Clothesline cities,
And temples on mountain retreats.
"High treason!" he repeated,
With insidious disbelief.
"That I were a Christ,
Born to some First Cause!"

Then the mired waters
Overflowed their banks,
And as he lay there,
Fingers of liquid heat
Closed in about his neck,
Burning off dead memories.
Sand and skin congealed
Blessedly, until he drowned,
Purified.

In five short breaths,
He was filtered back
To the river's other shore.
He had seen Eden
But was home once more,
A stranger in a stranger land
Than he'd ever known before,
Where a babe lay facedown,
Weeping.

By the manger, he placed
The mended tablets,
Which had washed up with him,
Whispering into the child's ears,
"Mercy and right reason
Shall be your crime. Tribunals
Shall sentence you for treason.
You'll be their only sinner,
My quiet Prince of Light."

Morning Rush Hour

The morning hour backs up,
Totters, spreads out,
One block at a time,
As ink on a mottled blotter.
Cars salted with frost
List along the street,
Precariously sliding in opposites
Like undone souls
Rushing toward resurrection.

Their breath depresses the air,
Disperses, and is lost,
Making room for newer exhaust.
I don't see cars, now,
On the tight-lipped thoroughfare
But a circus,
Whose light-footed elephants
Loiter in line, trunk to tail,
Or an endless assembly line,
Stalled by a power failure
At the traffic sign.
The sun teases a thousand glowering faces
As it dances from shadow to glass,
Cauterizing thoughts in antic frieze.

The Accomplishing

I

An eyeblink ten days long,
And all has gone from space to industry
As if winter's relinquishment
Were an act of generosity.
All of it, a child in bed: trees, nests,
Restive cocoons, buds tucked under pith,
Each species wrapped in warming, with care,
Sharing a million washes and hues.
This is the time for choosing.
Myriad reincarnations advertise themselves
Against a sky too veteran for surprise.
Unnumbered substances engender legions.
Infinite divinities explode. All the air
Is a miner on haunches by a stream,
Screening minerals through a leaky sieve.
Every odor, every color is a kite
Pasted upon a corrugated climate.
If there was a pause in the process
When the awful, cold air balked
And recognitions of another self
Gained definition, they did not know it
Or see it or feel or hear it happening.

II

The lilacs' purple-petaled cones
Postulate a queen's sweetest fragrance.
Even a vagrant blue jay strays to sniff
Before sifting away. In the rusted gutter
Above the eaves of this sleeping house,
Martins, starlings, and vicious wrens
Cease their vendettas to take note.
Tulips, tumid as guinea pigs, line walls
Where ivy begins its purblind ascent.
Boxwoods and hollies inflate with green
To hide the robin and mockingbird,
Whose mimetic activities deceive the ear.
Elms, sweet gums, expansive oaks, and
Tandem walnut trees that turret the front
*

Choke for the screaming growth,
And all is caught in furious frieze.
Everywhere, forsythias and dogwoods
Quilt collages no museum could frame.
Nowhere can the curious eye find rest
From redbuds and white apple trees,
Whose supple puberty defies violation.
This is the haughtiest season of all.

III

Only the mimosa and three magnolia trees
That border the moss-fatted patio
Decline this festivaled invitation.
The four are whores poised nakedly
In the face of boisterous neighbors
Who recline in overstuffed chairs
On a porticoed porch overlooking summer.
They stand in alien irrelation
In this warming northern clime:
Brown the magnolias' life, bleak
The Delta mistress who knows time
Does penance to her coquettishness.
Perhaps they know this moiling thickness,
This quick, wet seething of soil and air,
This crowded sharing of noisy space,
Is but fanfare for the marathon
They'll spend three months running.

IV

The community glowers at their sterility,
Mocks their recalcitrant inconsistency,
Their apparent insensitivity to the hour.
They withstand these evanescent abuses,
Unable to liberate collective knowledge
Or inculcate measured proprieties
They have gained for the going ahead.
This is a cruel place for the few
Who patiently await their appointed time.
Yet they alone, for the gaudy revellers,
*

Will explode into the mildest whites
And blessed scented rose, the softest pods,
The strongest supple leaves of deepest green,
When, in June, the nights catch fire,
July singes lawns and limbs like skin
Roasted over a charcoal grate,
And August suffocates the most chronic weeds.

BIOGRAPHICAL NOTE

Louis Daniel Brodsky was born in St. Louis, Missouri, in 1941, where he attended St. Louis Country Day School. After earning a B.A., magna cum laude, at Yale University in 1963, he received an M.A. in English from Washington University in 1967 and an M.A. in Creative Writing from San Francisco State University the following year.

Mr. Brodsky is the author of thirty-five volumes of poetry, five of which have been published in French by Éditions Gallimard. His poems have appeared in *Harper's*, *Southern Review*, *Texas Quarterly*, *National Forum*, *Ariel*, *American Scholar*, *Kansas Quarterly*, Ball State University's *Forum*, *New Welsh Review*, *Cimarron Review*, *Orbis*, and *Literary Review*, as well as in five editions of the *Anthology of Magazine Verse and Yearbook of American Poetry*.

Also available from **Time Being Books**

LOUIS DANIEL BRODSKY

You Can't Go Back, Exactly

The Thorough Earth

Four and Twenty Blackbirds Soaring

Mississippi Vistas: Volume One of *A Mississippi Trilogy*

Falling from Heaven: Holocaust Poems of a Jew and a Gentile
(with William Heyen)

Forever, for Now: Poems for a Later Love

Mistress Mississippi: Volume Three of *A Mississippi Trilogy*

A Gleam in the Eye: Poems for a First Baby

Gestapo Crows: Holocaust Poems

The Capital Café: Poems of Redneck, U.S.A.

Disappearing in Mississippi Latitudes: Volume Two of *A Mississippi Trilogy*

Paper-Whites for Lady Jane: Poems of a Midlife Love Affair

The Complete Poems of Louis Daniel Brodsky: Volume One, 1963–1967

HARRY JAMES CARGAS (editor)

Telling the Tale: A Tribute to Elie Wiesel on the Occasion of His 65th Birthday — Essays, Reflections, and Poems

JUDITH CHALMER

Out of History's Junk Jar: Poems of a Mixed Inheritance

GERALD EARLY

How the War in the Streets Is Won: Poems on the Quest of Love and Faith

ALBERT GOLDBARTH

A Lineage of Ragpickers, Songpluckers, Elegiasts & Jewelers: Selected Poems of Jewish Family Life (1973–1995)

ROBERT HAMBLIN

From the Ground Up: Poems of One Southerner's Passage to Adulthood

WILLIAM HEYEN

Erika: Poems of the Holocaust

Falling from Heaven: Holocaust Poems of a Jew and a Gentile
(with Louis Daniel Brodsky)

Pterodactyl Rose: Poems of Ecology

Ribbons: The Gulf War — A Poem

The Host: Selected Poems, 1965–1990

TED HIRSCHFIELD
German Requiem: Poems of the War and the Atonement of a Third
Reich Child

VIRGINIA V. JAMES HLAVSA
Waking October Leaves: Reanimations by a Small-Town Girl

RODGER KAMENETZ
The Missing Jew: New and Selected Poems

NORBERT KRAPF
Somewhere in Southern Indiana: Poems of Midwestern Origins
Blue-Eyed Grass: Poems of Germany

ADRIAN LOUIS
Blood Thirsty Savages

GARDNER McFALL
The Pilot's Daughter

JOSEPH MEREDITH
Hunter's Moon: Poems from Boyhood to Manhood

BEN MILDER
The Good Book Says . . . : Light Verse to Illuminate the Old Testament

TIME BEING BOOKS
POETRY IN SIGHT AND SOUND
St. Louis, Missouri

FOR OUR FREE CATALOG OR TO ORDER
(800) 331-6605 • FAX: (888) 301-9121
http://www.bookworld.com/timebeing/